The Value of Sport

This concise and thought-provoking book examines the myths and realities surrounding the value of sport. It asks a fundamental question: what is it about sport that leads to grand claims about its supposed capacity to do so many good things for society?

Examining the evidence from sport around the world, at all levels, the book challenges the commonly held, uncritical assumptions about the value of sport. It looks closely at the claims that sport is likely to improve physical and mental health and social cohesion or that there are demonstrable economic benefits to local communities and positive legacy effects from international sporting events and elite athletic successes. Adopting a value-adding perspective, the book argues that governments and policy-makers must strip away the myths, be more critical in their thinking, and recognise the counter-argument that sport is also associated with negative effects, whether that's the opportunity costs of allocating public funds to sport or the social harms for which sport can be responsible, such as drug use, violence, misogyny, racism, injury, or abuse. The book presents a broad-based framework for assessing the value of sport that focuses on citizen well-being, where a mix of collaborative public and self-organised regulation is used to help sport avoid becoming an infamous case study in market failure.

Presenting fresh thinking on an important topic, this book is essential reading for anybody working in sport policy, sport governance, sport management, or wider public policy spaces.

Bob Stewart is a professor and policy consultant in the not-for-profit sector, having had 25 years of experience teaching and researching in the sport management field of study at Victoria University in Melbourne, Australia, where he was the sport management programme director.

Aaron C.T. Smith is Professor and Director of the University of Canberra Research Institute for Sport and Exercise (UC-RISE) and Professor of Sport Business and Innovation in the Institute for Sport Business at Loughborough University London.

Sport Business Insights

Series Editors
Aaron C.T. Smith, Loughborough University, UK
Constantino Stavros, RMIT University, Australia

Sport Business Insights is a series that aims to cut through the clutter, providing concise and relevant introductions to an array of contemporary topics related to the business of sport. Readers – including passionate practitioners, curious consumers and sport students alike – will discover direct and succinct volumes, carefully curated to present a useful blend of practice and theory. In a highly readable format, and prepared by leading experts, this series shines a spotlight on subjects of currency in sport business, offering a systematic guide to critical concepts and their practical application.

Available in this series:

Sport Branding Insights
Constantino Stavros and Aaron C.T. Smith

Sport Sponsorship Insights
Norm O'Reilly, Gashaw Abeza and Mark Harrison

Esports Insights
Emily Hayday, Holly Collison-Randall and Sarah Kelly

Stadia Naming Rights in Sport
Leah Gillooly, Terry Eddy and Dominic Medway

Sport Governance Insights
Christos Anagnostopoulos, Dimitra Papadimitriou, Terri Byers and Grzegorz Botwina

Positive Sport Organizational Insights
Minjung Kim, Brent D. Oja and Christos Anagnostopoulos

The Value of Sport Insights
Bob Stewart and Aaron C.T. Smith

The Value of Sport

Insights

Bob Stewart and Aaron C.T. Smith

LONDON AND NEW YORK

First published 2025
by Routledge
4 Park Square, Milton Park, Abingdon, Oxon OX14 4RN

and by Routledge
605 Third Avenue, New York, NY 10158

Routledge is an imprint of the Taylor & Francis Group, an informa business

British Library Cataloguing-in-Publication Data
A catalogue record for this book is available from the British Library

ISBN: 978-1-032-90289-0 (hbk)
ISBN: 978-1-032-90291-3 (pbk)
ISBN: 978-1-003-54693-1 (ebk)

DOI: 10.4324/9781003546931

Typeset in Times New Roman
by KnowledgeWorks Global Ltd.

Contents

List of Tables

1 The Value of Sport

Questioning the Value of Sport

If you were to ask a typical citizen to comment on sport's ability to make the world a better place, they would most probably say that it does. There are many good reasons for responding in this way. The 2024 Paris Olympic and Paralympics Games were a raging success, with millions of television viewers around the world mesmerised by the colour, excitement, and drama that relentlessly unfolded. To put it colloquially, the vibe was good. But sport does not always deliver socially beneficial outcomes. In many instances, it can produce significant social problems, with violence, injury, and other forms of harm following in its wake. There are consequently grounds for claiming that sport is an overrated institution that takes as much as it gives. So, what, exactly, is the truth of the matter, and how might we best discover it?

This book is about making sense of sport by critically assessing the contribution it makes to the well-being of citizens. There are various ways of approaching this somewhat daunting task, with each approach focussing on a specific measurement tool. Social utility is one measure,[1] together with the more generalised concepts of quality of life and standard of living. One of the most enduring indicators of how well a society satisfies the aspirations of its citizens is the 'common good,'[2] which aims to measure the capacity of an institution, facility, or product to serve a 'common interest.' The common interest can revolve around things like economic security, social connectedness, educational opportunity, an egalitarian public health network, and an ethos of safety, liberty, and social justice.'

For this book, we have decided to utilise two related measures: the first is public value[3] and the second is capital-building capability,[4] otherwise known as capital accumulation. They have been selected because they not only have a strong theoretical base but also encompass a broad range of social impacts, economic benefits, cultural enhancements, and environmental improvements.

DOI: 10.4324/9781003546931-1

Structure, Approach, and Argument

There are millions of people around the world who believe sport contributes as much or more to the well-being and life satisfaction of citizens than any other institution, industry, or enterprise. This is a bold statement since educationalists, artists, and religious leaders have also made strong claims about their own institutional or ideological ability to do the same, and in many instances do it better. This begs the question: what is it about sport that leads to the grand assertion about its supposed capacity to do so many good things for society?

The justification goes as follows: sport not only delivers intrinsic pleasure, excitement, and moments of joy but also provides a vast array of positive 'spinoffs' that add something to society. These spinoffs include a strong ethical mindset, increased self-esteem, greater emotional resilience, improved educational attainment, the creation of positive role models, social cohesion, crime reduction, more connected communities, improvements in physical and mental health, increased productivity at work, an economic benefit to local communities, and a longer, more satisfying, and happier lifespan.

It is even suggested that whenever waves of national pride wash over citizens – having watched 'their' athletes perform well on the international sporting stage – there will be a legacy effect that can last for years. Being inspired to participate as a player in spaces created because of these international successes is a case in point.

But there is also a counter-narrative at play: most of the spinoffs that sport's proponents claim for its participants are little more than comforting myths. They make intuitive sense since there is always some anecdotal support for them, and a good story to tell. However, when the research is done and the findings are in, many of them do not stack up to the test of objective evidence. There is also a more serious problem to consider when making this counter-argument. It has to do with all the costs and harms incurred when people engage in sport, and which the myths frequently camouflage. For example, the time and money spent on playing and watching sport, buying equipment, securing club membership, and travelling to and from venues is a very small tip of a problematic iceberg. There are also opportunity costs that accompany sport where resources might have contributed towards the greater good in some other way, like spending directly on preventative health and social equity programmes.

In addition, just below the surface of sport there is a layer of drug use, violence, bribery, corruption, and match-fixing, and below that is a disturbing level of misogyny, homophobia, racism, and frightening misbehaviour by officials, parents, and fans. Deeper again is the taken-for-granted but increasingly heavy societal burden of dealing with body and head injury, mental illness, and related disorders.

These competing narratives raise the next question: is sport a key to a good society and thus deserves every dollar it gets from government, sponsors, and fans, or is it an overrated institution that not only fails to deliver on many of its spinoff promises but also in the process creates widespread levels of social chaos, physical harm, and psychological distress?

We argue that unless governments and sport policy-makers intervene by first, stripping away the myths of sport rather than repeating them at every opportunity, and second, critically re-visiting the regulatory regimes that are supposed to ensure sport is a safe space for all, sport's contribution to the well-being of citizens will be questionable at best, if not acutely problematic. And, if things get worse, sport faces the prospect of becoming an infamous case study in market failure.

We consequently suggest that sport policy-makers need a fresh way of evaluating sport's public value and capital-building capability that not only celebrates sport's achievements but also acknowledges the costs, harms, and destructive practices (some of which are inevitable and many that are not) that occur along the way. The book culminates in a consideration of alternative frameworks for assessing the value of contemporary sport.

Finally, within the previous constraints, the book wraps up its analysis by offering a sustainable way forward for sport through collaborative and self-organised regulation, as well as a refreshed narrative that better fits our challenging and constantly changing times.

In short, this book reveals a significant sporting paradox which governments need to understand when working out how to get the best from sport. Sport is, by its very nature, a risky enterprise, and whenever someone attempts to take all the potential harm and danger away, it usually results in something less spectacular, less alluring, and less meaningful to its fans and followers. While many critics will say that sport's core problem is that it is too competitive, too combative, and too gendered, this book examines the counterclaim that these three factors are the key to the essence of sport and its continued popularity

This book will appeal to students, scholars, and practitioners who want to dig deeper into both the heroic realm of sport and its harsh realities. It offers a framework for thinking about enhancing sport's positive outcomes while reducing its negative ones. A little more presumptuously, the book will – by providing an evidence-based framework – assist policy analysts and politicians in delivering government programmes that not only make us better off but also do it efficiently and fairly.

Chapter Breakdown

Chapter 2 introduces readers to the complexities of sport. It begins by noting the many societal changes that have taken place over the last 50 years or so and the ways in which sport has adapted to them. It then uses this turbulent context to examine the nature and essence of sport and what makes it different from play, games, and recreation. It also discusses the factors that motivate people to engage in sport while noting the distinction between playing sport and watching others play.

Chapter 3 reveals two competing narratives that aim to explain the ways in which sport works in practice. It begins by discussing how – for most people – sport does everything asked of it and more. It not only makes them happier, healthier, and more connected to their communities but also builds character, improves educational outcomes, and gives adolescents a sound ethical framework for making their way through the world. It also presents a counter narrative that challenges this view. For sceptics and critics, sport is socially destructive, since it encourages questionable and selfish practices, provides fertile ground for match-fixing, fuels addiction to illicit drug use, exacerbates gambling problems, heightens the risk of injury, and creates dysfunctional cultures embedded with prejudices around gender, race, sexuality, and disability.

Chapter 4 revisits our key concepts, with public value and capital accumulation front and centre. Our aim here is to provide a more detailed historical context, while also explaining their importance in ensuring a systematic analysis of our findings. We also wanted to put a bit more intellectual meat on our conceptual skeleton.

Chapter 5 frames sport in terms of its public value, questioning whether it possesses a special ability to make the world better, or is instead an overrated institution that delivers as much mayhem as it does joy. We identified 15 propositions about sport's ability to do good things for society and matched them against the result of relevant research. In most cases, the propositions were problematic with some of the evidence undermining their credibility.

Chapter 6 unpacks the capital value of sport, asking whether sport adds to the capital stocks of society, or is it progressively stripping away some of its most precious forms of capital, be it economic, social, physical, psychological, or moral. It does this by looking at the research and asking if the findings match the claims about sport's ability to do good things for society and its citizens. The findings were more equivocal than many readers would have expected.

Chapter 7 addresses the findings from Chapters 5 and 6 and their implications for the challenges sport currently faces. It reveals many strengths of sport while also highlighting its weaknesses and failings. It suggests that many of its failings arise from regulatory regimes that look good on paper but do not deliver on their promises. Chapter 7 goes on to explore the ways sport policy-makers might more sharply identify conduct that fails the public interest test, but also assist in formulating a regulatory mix that can maximise sport's value, strengthen its capital-building capability, and, in turn, enhance citizen well-being.

Chapter 8 looks to the future of sport and proposes what needs to be done to make sure sport builds more public value and societal capital while minimising the ever-increasing risks and harms that make it potentially costly. It confirms that sport has been organised around a bundle of myths that sometimes have little resemblance to reality. It also observes that sport has hidden many of its problematic practices from the public gaze. Chapter 8 goes on to suggest that despite all the risks and harms, sport delivers enormous joy and pleasure to its followers. It meets many needs, some of which are difficult to pin down and superficially materialist, but others which are etched in the brain from tens of thousands of years celebrating – and sometimes worshipping – those who protected tribal members from starvation and marauding enemies.

When it comes to recommending a new course of action for sport, Chapter 8 observes that while each sport has its own special qualities, there are some broad organising principles that, if implemented properly, can improve social, economic, and cultural outcomes. They include grass-roots activism, more transparent and accountable governance, collaborative engagement with key stakeholders, incentives to change behaviour, more vigilant forms of self-regulation, and the targeted use of command-and-control external regulation that wields heavy sanctions for transgressions.

Chapter 8 also examines more radical options, including the redesign of body contact sports to eliminate head-on collisions, the introduction of heavy penalties for any form of referee or player abuse, the experience of chronic concussion as a reason for de-registering players, the instigation of government takeovers of sporting competitions that have engaged in criminal activity, and handing out significant penalties to clubs and teams whose members engage in anti-social behaviour. At the same time, Chapter 8 highlights the practical obstacles that make some of these interventions not only implausible but also dangerous.

Notes

1 A useful explanation of social utility from a public health perspective is provided in Kathryn MacKay (2018). Perspectives: Utility and justice in public health, *Journal of Public Health*, 40 (3): 413–418. For a recent application of social utility theory to the world of sport and recreation, see B. Liu, Y. Chen and M. Xiao (2020). The social utility and health benefits for older adults of amenity buildings in China's urban parks: A Nanjing case study, *International Journal of Environmental Research and Public Health*, 17 (20): Online publication

2 Marcus Raskin (1986). *The Common Good: Its Politics, Policies and Philosophies*, Routledge and Kegan, 25.

3 Public Value was given international currency with the publication of Mark Moore (1995). *Creating Public Value: Strategic Management in Government*, Harvard University Press. Additional analysis and interpretation have been undertaken by Martin Cole and Greg Parston (2006). *Unlocking Public Value: A New Model for Achieving High Performance in Public Service Organisations*, John Wiley and Sons; Janine O'Flynn (2021). Where to for public value? Taking stock and moving

on, *International Journal of Public Administration*, 44 (10): 867–877; and Rick Wylie [ed.] (2021). *Public Value Management: Institutional Design and Decision for the Common Good,* Rowman & Littlefield

4 If you want to find out more about the concept of capital and how it has evolved over the last 150 years or so, see Baldwin Ranson (1987). The institutionalist theory of capital formation, *Journal of Economic Issues*, 21 (3): 1265–1278; Amartya Sen (1987). Editorial - Human capital and human capability, *World Development*, 25 (12): Online publication; and Martha Nussbaum (2011). *Creating Capabilities: The Human Development Approach*, Belknap Press.

2 The Complexities of Sport

Setting the Scene

Over recent times, making sense of sport has become an increasingly complex task. Like every other social institution over the last 50 years or so, it has been radically transformed by society's furious journey along the information superhighway towards the AI autobahn. The forces for change, be they economic, social, or cultural, have been both subtle and brutal.

It all began with postmaterialism, a term coined by American social scientist Ronald Inglehart in his seminal 1977 publication, *The Silent Revolution: Changing Values and Political Styles Among Western Publics*. Inglehart found that prior to the 1970s, most western societies prioritised materialist values such as economic growth, physical security, self-discipline, and the maintenance of social order. But during the 1970s a postmaterialist ethos emerged, which gave greater weight to social issues such as environmental protection, freedom of speech, self-expression, cultural diversity, gender equality, and social justice.[1] In 2008, Inglehart provided an update which confirmed this postmaterialist values shift. But he also acknowledged that it had created widespread anxiety for many people, who having cast aside old traditions and taken for granted norms and customs, found themselves facing a crisis of identity.[2]

Digitisation followed hot on the heels of postmaterialism, and its implications were quickly felt. Wim Westera, in his 2012 book, *The Digital Turn: How the Internet Transforms Our Existence*, found that online experiences delivered a fundamentally different mode of being that produced a detached, and distorted view of the 'real' world. Westera was concerned that online obsessions, especially amongst adolescents, could lead to 'fake conversations,' a fragmented identity, a plethora of 'virtual friends,' fewer real friends, an overall loss of face-to-face social engagement, and in the most serious of cases, a disengagement with life at large.[3] But he also acknowledged that this new digitised world had sparked a global communication revolution where the idea of mass communication had reached its zenith, and anyone with anything

DOI: 10.4324/9781003546931-2

to say, however mundane, crass, offensive, or bizarre, could reach an international audience.

Finally, we also entered a period of hyper-modernity, which was the culmination of a shift from modernity during the 1950s and 1960s to a more radicalised and fractured world that emerged during the 1970s and 1980s. According to Gilles Lipovetsky[4] in his 2005 publication, *Hypermodern Times*, midway through the 1990s – which coincided with the early internet and world-wide web – Western society entered an 'age of excess' where 'rampant individualism' and the 'commercialisation of lifestyle' followed the breakdown of traditional hierarchies and authority relations. Beliefs, attitudes, and behaviours were no longer constrained by the social and moral demands of the family, the Church, and the state, and gave way to a smorgasbord of lifestyle and leisure options. One of these options centred on the 'self' and how to construct an identity that was no longer only ascribed by virtue of family backgrounds, religious affiliations, cultural traditions, or occupations. According to Lipovetsky, this vacuum was not only filled by hedonistic consumption and marketised leisure but also created feelings of emptiness and anxiety.

John Ebert and Brian Culkin in their 2019 book, *Hypermodernity & The End of the World*, were saying much the same thing, but with the volume turned up. Like Lipovetsky, they mapped its origins, with the second half of the 1990s marking its beginnings. According to Ebert and Culkin, this revolutionary landscape was in large part shaped by the neo-liberal processes of globalisation, where free trade, waves of migration from poor to rich nations, and a super-fast international communications network changed the ways in which people moved through the world. This combination of neo-liberalism and radically enhanced computational technologies delivered massive levels of personal freedom and autonomy but also de-centred people's sense of stability. It was also associated with a 'pandemic of narcissism,' the emergence of Donald Trump as a significant political player and disrupter, the 'dissolution of community,' and the 'erosion of cultural values.'[5]

Sport was reshaped by these monumental changes in society and subsequently became part of the global entertainment industry. It employed millions of people to design and build stadiums, organise events, coach players, and condition athletes at the same time as paying some players massive amounts of money to engage in various types of marketable physical contests. Sport also became the lifeblood of the media, both hard copy and digital. By matching audiences to advertisers and people to events and happenings, it created a previously unimaginable network of sports-talk and delivered huge online sport-related archives for viewing and sharing. Community sport was also seduced by the world of commerce and consumerism, where amateurism increasingly meant nothing, winning meant everything, and letting the world know about it via social media was mandatory.

Like its commercial and cultural surroundings, sport had contradictions galore, where memorable experiences were juxtaposed against ephemeral 'fillers,' the aesthetics of games clashed with their brutality, a finely tuned body became a major disability at the drop of an injury, banal lulls filled the gaps between spectacular incidents, and player and fan despondency followed joy like night followed day. At the same time, sport had never been so eclectic, so accessible, or so popular, with most of the world's major festivals being sport related.[6]

We converge on the question: in this constantly changing, globalised world, where disruption is lurking at every corner of the planet, just how important is sport in the lives of ordinary citizens, and has it shaped their lives for better or for worse? To answer this question, we will critically assess its public value and capital-building capability, which is a pretentious way of asking how it has impacted the well-being, living standards, and quality of life of societies and their citizens. However, before we get into the analysis, we need to introduce some pivotal concepts and define a few key terms, including what we mean by sport itself.

Understanding the Boundaries of 'Sport'

Sport has long been a pivotal leisure experience, having provided many material benefits as well as giving meaning to life. However, defining sport is complex as it varies amongst individuals. Some may not consider horse racing or gym workouts as sports, while others do. Even video gaming and e-sport, with their massive markets, are considered sports by some. The proposal to include chess in the Olympics raised questions about the physicality aspect of sports. As it turns out, the concept of sport is elusive and subjective. Plato's idea of 'Forms' suggests that the true nature of things, including sport, can only be understood through deep contemplation.[7]

The etymology of 'sport' traces back to the 15th century, meaning 'to take pleasure' or 'amuse oneself.'[8] Over time, it evolved to describe physical games. Sport also embodies elements of play; an instinctive, unstructured activity primarily for enjoyment. Scholars like Johan Huizinga[9] and Roger Caillois[10] have explored the concept of play, emphasising its voluntary, spontaneous, and creative nature.

Sport, while containing elements of play, is distinct due to its physicality, competitiveness, and structured rules. Bernard Suit[11] argued that physical games without winners or losers are not sports. Thus, activities like surfboard riding for fun or lifesaving remain recreational. The amount of physical effort required for an activity to be considered a sport is also disputed. French anthropologist Claude Lévi Strauss suggested that not all games aim for a win, citing examples of ceremonial games amongst indigenous communities.[12] These games, while physical, do not have outright winners and served mainly cultural and ritualistic purposes.

Towards a Definition of Sport

The definition of sport continues to be debated, with some advocating for a broad inclusion of any physical activity. This inclusive view, however, risks overestimating participation in organised sports and overlooking casual physical activities. The Australian Bureau of Statistics (ABS) has a commendable record of tracking the evolution of sports, scrutinising its ties with leisure and physicality, and striving to better classify the myriad leisure activities that require some form of physical effort.[13] It is now widely agreed that sport is one of many forms of physical activity that enhance people's enjoyment, purpose, and productivity in life.

Using the ABS's frameworks, sports analysts have employed 'physical activity' as a comprehensive term to encompass three functional categories. First, sport, which is characterised as participation in a structured, competitive game or contest that necessitates a degree of physical effort and the application of one or more motor skills, with the objective being triumph. The second category of physical activity is exercise, which consists of structured routines of repetitive physical movements aimed at increasing muscle mass and tone, enhancing strength, boosting fitness levels, reducing body fat, and improving agility and flexibility. The objective here is self-enhancement. The third category is active recreation, which includes less structured activities that can still be quite physically intense. These can range from a lengthy stroll in the park, lap swimming, a beach day, or a leisurely bike ride. The objective here can vary from stress alleviation to companionship or simply getting out of the house. Active recreation also encompasses outdoor adventure, which often takes individuals into wild bushland environments. In this scenario, the objective is to not only appreciate the splendour of nature but also to develop mental resilience or reduce stress.

Sport is one of many forms of physical activity conducted in a leisure, or non-work, environment; we can therefore differentiate between physical activity performed in the workplace and physical activity carried out in a leisure setting. Occupations such as plumbing and bricklaying are highly physical, while an office job can be entirely sedentary. However, both are forms of work. While some individuals may spend most of their time working, others will devote most of their time to leisure activities. While leisure time can be a serious endeavour for many individuals most of the time, a significant proportion may choose to do very little, even when time is abundant. It is perfectly acceptable to spend one's time doing nothing. As it turns out, sleeping and daydreaming consume more time than any other domestic activity.

We have so far outlined the unique blend of elements that distinguish sport from other leisure activities, but these do not delve into its core essence, or its ideal Form, as Plato's ancient Greece would term it. The quintessential vision of sport, which the Greeks believed they had encapsulated in the Olympic Games more than 2000 years ago, remains elusive. So, where do we start?

An easy but good first step is to identify what sport isn't. For starters, most of our leisure activities have little connection to sport, whether it's watching TV, posting on socials, streaming videos, reading, socialising, or playing e-games. Sport also has minimal relevance to the workplace, although it has recently adopted several work-like characteristics. As previously mentioned, play is now only a peripheral aspect of sport. When defining sport in its purest form, the ancient Greeks were largely accurate in stating that it's all about competition. Historians, anthropologists, and evolutionary psychologists have further added physicality, skill, power, and finesse to this definition. Despite a few rare instances of competitions without winners, victory is the goal, demonstrating a participant's ability to run faster, jump higher, throw further, and make an opponent submit quicker. As previously emphasised, a legitimate sport requires organisation, meaning that competitions are conducted under a mutually agreed set of rules and overseen by trustworthy and impartial officials.

This leads us to Table 2.1, which provides further insights into the fundamental nature of sport by constructing a formal eight-category typology of leisure experiences.

Our categorisation of leisure activities places the origins of sport as far removed from work as possible. Like paid work, it is firmly situated within an organisational context. It is not a random or spontaneous event, but rather the outcome of a desire for structure, boundaries, and consistency. It involves a serious competition where winners and losers are clearly declared, with winners being hailed as heroes and losers commended for their valiant efforts. Lastly, athletic physicality is a must, with the body being pushed to its limits and significant energy expended to overcome the hurdles on the path to victory.

By exploring different pathways within Table 2.1, we arrive at scenarios that allow us to redefine and categorise sport in a novel way, depicted in Table 2.2.

This template's worth lies in its ability to extend beyond mere leisure classification and stimulate thoughts about a 'sports hierarchy' using the ideal Forms approach, as hinted at in Table 2.2. The ideal Form is undoubtedly found in the LPOC category, as all other categories fall short of perfection.

Table 2.1 Twenty-first Century Leisure Categories

Category	*Combination of 'cells'*
1	Leisure, physical, organised, recreational (LPOR)
2	Leisure, physical, organised, competitive (LPOC)
3	Leisure, physical, unorganised, recreational (LPUR)
4	Leisure, physical, unorganised, competitive (LPUC)
5	Leisure, sedentary, organised, recreational (LSOR)
6	Leisure, sedentary, organised, competitive (LSOC)
7	Leisure, sedentary, unorganised, recreational (LSUR)
8	Leisure, sedentary, unorganised, competitive (LSUC)

Table 2.2 Framework for Re-categorising Leisure Pursuits

Combination of 'cells'	*Acronym*	*Examples*
Leisure, physical, organised, competitive	LPOC	Mixed martial arts, boxing, football, track and field, tennis, gymnastics, ten-pin bowling
Leisure, physical, organised, recreational	LPOR	Pilates class, personal training session, bushwalking club activities
Leisure, physical, unorganised, competitive	LPUC	Pick-up game of cricket, impromptu snow-skiing contest
Leisure, physical, unorganised, recreational	LPUR	Surfing, casual walking, lap swimming
Leisure, sedentary, organised, competitive	LSOC	Chess competitions, e-sports
Leisure, sedentary, organised, recreational	LSOR	Book reading club activity, participation in foreign language class, eating out
Leisure, sedentary, sedentary, competitive	LSUC	Spontaneous game of cards with friends
Leisure, sedentary, unorganised, recreational	LSUR	Sunbaking in a backyard, playing solitaire, daydreaming, resting

Categories LPOR, LPUC, and LPUR deviate from conventional sports perceptions as they lack the critical features. The LSOC category is intriguing as it includes activities like chess and e-sport, helping resolve disputes about their inclusion in the sports realm. However, even the most creative and nimble mental acrobatics could not incorporate activities from categories LSOR, LSUR, and LSUC into the sports family.

In essence, recent efforts to expand the boundaries of sport often hinge on the generous – and some might argue, strange – idea that a game or contest doesn't need a physical component to be classified as a sport. Alternatively, it's suggested that sport doesn't need to be competitive or contest based. We strongly disagree. In our sports world, the physical contest is fundamental. Without it, it's more about games and play. While games and play undoubtedly bring immense joy and pleasure to participants, they should not be viewed as sports due to the absence of a physical contest.

Simultaneously, the LPOC lineage allows us to establish a more nuanced hierarchy of 'perfection' within this sports categorisation. In other words, different sports could be placed at different points on the perfection scale. An ancient Greek sports purist might argue, for example, that contests where players demonstrate their skills and physical prowess in time and space separate from their competitors are subpar. To achieve the highest standard, contestants would have to share the same space at the same time.

Under this premise, combat and collision sports top the sports perfection pyramid as they involve close physical contact for extended periods. Boxing, wrestling, mixed martial arts, and various team ball sports are prime examples. This finding echoes Desmond Morris,[14] David Sansone,[15] Panos Valavanis,[16] and Michael Lombardo,[17] who each made similar points about the depth of meaning for different sports and the ensuing popularity. In other words, (1) one-on-one combat sports and (2) team sports (which not only replicate the skills needed for hunting and warfare success but also involve body contact and victory or defeat as the metaphorical kill) will always attract the largest crowds.

Some forms of road cycling and long-distance running might also qualify, but anything else would be imperfect. And, at first glance, running, swimming, rowing, and canoeing events, where all performances occur simultaneously, would also meet the pure-sport test. However, participants must maintain their distance by competing in their own space or 'lane.' So, while these sports allow for sharing the same time, they deny participants the same space. The perfectibility of sport is further reduced when participants in the same event perform not only in separate spaces but also at staggered times. Sports like gymnastics, skiing, shooting, archery, throwing activities, and jumping events fall into this category.

In our model, a sport's perfectibility is further reduced when winners are determined based on subjective judgment. Combat sports and racing events have clear winners, as do team sports. But sports like gymnastics, ice-dancing, skateboarding, diving, synchronised swimming, 'breaking,' and sometimes boxing and fencing are devalued by disputes over who was, in fact, the best performer. In these cases, victory is largely determined by subjective evaluation and all the biases and prejudices that accompany it. This is particularly true for sports competitions where winners are decided based on artistic beauty and aesthetic appeal, where 'technical' judgments are made about the performance quality by expert officials. In the worst-case scenarios, judges may be bribed to fabricate a result, which completely undermines the contest's legitimacy. In these cases, any notion of perfection vanishes without a trace.

Considering the above discussion, we believe it makes sense to reassemble the LPOC category as a four-part hierarchical classification that has total perfectibility at the apex and heavily diminished perfectibility at the base. It can be modelled as follows in Table 2.3.

While all sports are, by definition, real and have a degree of perfection embedded in them, under our model, some are more perfect than others. This raises two important questions: first, do sports deemed to be the most perfect create better societal outcomes than those which do not? Or whether in fact the opposite is the case. Second, having found the answer, what should we do about it?

We've re-thought the criteria that distinguish a pastime from a sport, pinpointing the core of sports and outlining its limits. However, we've noticed

Table 2.3 A Model of Sport Perfection for LPOC Sports

Features	*Examples*	*Features highly valued*	*Level of idealised perfection*
Type 1: Constant and close physical contact in common space and time for extended periods; victory is objectively measured	Boxing, Wresting, Mixed Martial Arts, Football, Fencing	Courage, Resilience, Heroism, Elite Performance	Absolute Perfection
Type 2: Participants maintain distance but performed concurrently; victory is objectively measured	Running, Equestrian (Cross Country)	Strength, Skill	Marginally Imperfect
Type 3: Participants perform not only in separate spaces but also at staggered times; victory is objectively measured	Archery, Shooting	Skill	Slightly Imperfect
Type 4: Participants perform not only in separate spaces but also at staggered times; victory is subjectively measured	Gymnastics, Diving, Equestrian (Dressage)	Skill, Aesthetic Appeal	Moderately Imperfect

that while the core of sports remains constant, its boundaries are ever-evolving. This has led us to question whether the redefinition of sports could potentially undermine the positive societal impact of traditional sports.

We've also ranked various sports against an ideal standard, identifying those that can be perfected and those that cannot. In our model, highly physical team sports that offer combat-like experiences in a unified space and time – such as football – sit at the top of the sports engagement pyramid. They embody the essence of sports and are therefore deemed perfect. Conversely, more aesthetic and less violent individual sports, where winners are subjectively judged across disjointed space and time – like gymnastics and diving – are positioned near the base as they capture only some aspects of sports' perfection.

The placement of e-sports remains a puzzle, considering its low level of physicality and whether a 'virtual' representation of participants competing in real-time qualifies as perfect. However, we also concede that by favouring intense sports over milder ones, our model endorses sports that could potentially cause significant harm due to their propensity for violence and injury. Our model also underestimates the social benefits derived from watching graceful movements performed by highly trained athletic bodies. We've also unintentionally landed in a predicament by favouring high-risk sports over low-risk ones. However, we pondered if this type of outcome could be rationalised by noting its popularity amongst sports fans. As we note in subsequent chapters, this idea comes with a fair bit of evidence, which implies that some sports can be popular while also diminishing their public value and capital-building capability. This becomes a cause for concern.

Notes

1 Ronald Inglehart (1977/2015). *The Silent Revolution: Changing Values and Political Styles Among Western Publics*, Princeton Legacy Library.
2 Ronald Inglehart (2008). Changing values among western publics from 1970 to 2006, *Western European Politics*, 31 (1–2): 130–146.
3 Wim Westera (2012). *The Digital Turn: How the Internet Transforms Our Existence*, AuthorHouse.
4 Gilles Lipovetsky 2005. *Hypermodern Times,* Translated by Andrew Brown, Polity.
5 John Ebert and Brian Culkin (2019). *Hypermodernity & The End of the World,* Independent Publishing.
6 Current television and on-line audience figures show that the Men's Cricket World Cup is the most watched sport event with an aggregated global viewing audience of around 6.6 billion. Following its wake is the Men's Soccer world Cup with 3.5 billion, the Summer Olympics with 3.0 billion, the Winter Olympics with 2.0 billion, the Women's Soccer World Cup with around 1.2 billion, and the Men's Rugby Union world Cup coming in at around 860 million. In contrast, the May 2023 coronation of Prince/King Charles attracted around 300 million pairs of eyeballs worldwide.
7 Arthur Herman (2013). *The Cave and the Light: Plato Versus Aristotle, and the Struggle for the Soul of Western Civilization*, Random House: 21.
8 On-line Etymological Dictionary (2022). www.etymonline.com/word/sport
9 Johan Huizinga (1950). *Homo Ludens: A Study of the Play Element in Culture*, Beacon Books.
10 Roger Caillois (1961). *Man, Play and Games,* Free Press of Glencoe: 10–11.
11 Bernard Suits (2007). The elements of sport, *Ethics in Sport*, 2 (3): 9–19.
12 Claude Lévi Straus (1962). *The Savage*, University of Chicago Press: 20. If you want to follow up on this case, more is revealed in K. Read (1959). Leadership and consensus in a New Guinea society, *American Anthropologist,* 61 (3): 425–430.
13 See for example ABS (1997). *4156.0 - Sport and Recreation: A Statistical Overview*, Australia. 4156.0 - Sport and Recreation: A Statistical Overview, Australia, 1997 (abs.gov.au); ABS (2012) *4156.0 - Sports and Physical Recreation: A Statistical Overview, Australia*. 4156.0 - Sports and Physical Recreation: A Statistical Overview, Australia, 2012 (abs.gov.au); ABS (2014). 4902.0 - *Australian Culture and Leisure Classifications*. 4902.0 - Australian Culture and Leisure Classifications, 2014 (Third Edition) (abs.gov.au); ABS (2014) *Perspectives on Sport*. Perspectives on Sport, April 2014 | Australian Bureau of Statistics (abs.gov.au)
14 Desmond Morris (1981). *The Soccer Tribe:* 10–23.
15 David Sansone (1988). *Greek Athletics and the Genesis of Sport,* University of California Press.
16 Panos Valavanis (2004). *Games and Sanctuaries in Ancient Greece*, The John Paul Getty Museum: 23.
17 Michael Lombardo (2012). On the evolution of sport, *Evolutionary Psychology*, 10 (1): 1–28.

3 Sport's Competing Narratives

The Value of Evidence

As we noted in the previous chapter, an enormous amount of research has been undertaken concerning the role sport plays in contemporary society. Theories from nearly every social science and humanities discipline – anthropology, economics, geography, history, management, philosophy, psychology, criminology, and sociology – have been used to find out where and when it originated, how it works, what it means, who wins, and who misses out. The medical and biological sciences have also ventured deeply into sport's impact on people's physical health, mental capacities, and social development. While few aspects of sport's multivarious impacts have been overlooked, they remain clouded by a lack of consensus on where the real truth lies.

Take, for example, sports' social impacts. In 2005 an analysis of sport's community connection and character-building was undertaken by Richard Bailey, culminating in a paper titled 'Evaluating the Relationship between Physical Education, Sport and Social Inclusion.'[1] Bailey noted that while well-organised sport programmes directed by well-trained staff delivered strongly positive impacts – including self-reliance, resilience, and social connectedness – he conceded that the benefits were not always evenly distributed, with already disadvantaged participants benefitting the least.

In another tantalising study, this time in 2017, Maurico Marques, Luciano Alencastro, and Rodrigo de Vargas invited sport coaches to reflect on the teaching of life skills to young people living in areas at risk of social exclusion. Nearly every coach highlighted the positive ways in which participants connected with the values of teamwork, discipline, and performance. Marques and his colleagues concluded that sport had a unique capacity to transform the lives of troubled adolescents.[2]

Jim Parry in his 2012 article, 'The Power of Sport in Peacemaking and Peacekeeping,' was equally effusive about sport's ability to do good.[3] According to Parry, sport's emphasis on 'equality, respect, mutuality, and other human rights values' made it a perfect fit for delivering peacemaking programmes. Parry admitted that sport itself was 'a form of violent conflict' and, at first

DOI: 10.4324/9781003546931-3

glance, 'antithetical to peace promotion.' He also acknowledged that 'competitive games' were contests where one person's abilities were tested against another's, which resulted in winners and losers. But, in Parry's estimation, winning did not have to be the overriding concern. Rather, it was possible to play to win while also valuing the 'opportunity to exercise speed, strength, determination, and skill.' Moreover, fair play in sport was not only a 'moral requirement' where rule adherence, acknowledgement of the spirit of sport, and fair-mindedness were front and centre, but it was also a 'logically necessary feature of successful engagement' where peaceful co-existence was the goal.

Parry's advocacy for sport as a tool for building peace – especially in developing nations – was the focus for Laura Zanotti, Max Stephenson Jr., and Marcy Schnitzer in their influential 2015 paper, 'Biopolitical and Disciplinary Peacebuilding: Sport, Reforming Bodies and Rebuilding Societies.'[4] The authors declared that sport was an ideal peacebuilding strategy because it not only aspired to 'change people's ways of living together' but was also a 'disciplinary technique applied to human bodies with a view to transforming the souls of individuals and moulding unruly subjects into good citizens.' They went on to note that the United Nations had embraced sport as a mechanism to mitigate conflict and encourage peace while also strengthening democratic processes.

Finally, a 2019 study of USA college students by Jeeyoon Kim and David Jeffrey had some fascinating things to say about the relationship between sport, well-being, and happiness.[5] They found that regular engagement in sport led to short-term improvements in happiness and 'life satisfaction.' In addition, this significant 'happiness yield' was associated with an increased sense of achievement, attachment, and belonging. Anticipating retorts that happiness was simply a function of doing well, Kim and Jeffrey confidently announced that changes in happiness scores had nothing to do with winning and losing.

This was all well and good, but a counter-narrative was gaining momentum as the 2000s unfolded. It maintained, in short, that sport was socially destructive. This was because it encouraged corrupt practices, provided fertile ground for match fixing, fuelled addiction to illicit drug use, exacerbated gambling problems, heightened the risk of injury, and created dysfunctional cultures embedded with prejudices around gender, race, sexuality, and disability.[6]

When it came to making the case for sport's problematic status, the work done by Eric Anderson and Adam White provided a good starting point. In their 2018 publication, *Sport, Theory and Social Problems: A Critical Introduction*, Anderson and White argued that sport was a hot bed of reactionary values, significant harms, and broad-based prejudices.[7] For instance, sport overly valued competition; it obsessed over obedience; it invited participants to accept, inflict, and enjoy violence; it utilised injuries – and concussions in particular – as badges of honour; it denied the rights of players (particularly young ones); it perpetuated class structures and the inequalities that went with them; it stratified men; it marginalised women; it subordinated racial minorities; and, finally, by utilising rigid stereotypes, it excluded those who were different and labelled them as dangerous 'others.' Jay Coakley's 2021 publication, *Sport in Society: Issues & Controversies*, covered a similar amount of critical terrain, including problems around socialisation, deviance, violence, class, ethnicity, race, disability, and gender. Coakley framed his introductory section with the concept of the 'Great Sport Myth,' which was embedded with individualistic notions of 'purity and goodness' and 'character.'[8] He proceeded to argue that this myth was indeed just a myth.

According to some critics, the harm sport caused went beyond the psychological, physical, and cultural and moved into the ideological and political. In his 2019 polemic, *Making Sport Great Again: The Uber-Sport Assemblage, Neoliberalism, and the Trump Conjuncture,* long-time critic of neo-liberal ideology and contemporary sport, David Andrews, argued that sport – especially at the professional level – had taken on a new and overwhelmingly oppressive cultural form that had moved well beyond its commercialised and corporatised structure of the 1990s and early 21st century.[9]

Andrews invented the term 'Uber-sport' as a way of describing big-time sport as it entered the 2020s. Accordingly, this phase of sport's evolution was fundamentally anti-democratic and unjust; it normalised patriarchy and was embedded with the structures, forces, and values of 19th-century discourses about English national character and appropriate moral behaviour. But, in Andrew's mind, sport was not only a reactionary institution. It had also become spectacularised, celebritised, and politicised.[10] It had become integrated into the capitalist economy and all its 'profit-driven structures and logics.' As a result, individuals were treated as a 'standardized part of the commodity producing machine.'[11] All the fun, spontaneity, and value had been squeezed out.

But just when readers might have thought that sport was beyond redemption, Andrews contrived that Uber-sport had the potential to develop a progressive 'liberatory politics' which countered, rather than validated, the established order. In the final chapter of *Making Sport Great Again,* Andrews reflected on how it may be possible to 'extricate uber-sport from its reactionary and regressive political functioning.' Something positive could be achieved if every socially progressive citizen (especially educators) could help de-articulate Uber-sport from its current neoliberal, meritocratic, and authoritarian populist mooring, and re-articulate it to progressive politics as a 'fully emancipatory and actualizing institution.'[12]

Andrews left the detail of how this would be operationalised for others to sort out. But Munene Mwaniki, an American sport analysist, tried to fill the gap by suggesting that 'socially conscious political actors' engineer some sort of grassroots Marxist-Leninist project as part of a 'revolutionary class struggle.'[13] Exactly what that meant for the likes of leading American football teams like the Dallas Cowboys and precociously talented tennis players like Iga Świątek remained unspecified.

Such criticism is not new. It goes back to the 1970s when American sociologist, Harry Edwards, argued that sport was far removed from 'play, fun and games.' It has assumed, no less, the character of an 'occupational endeavour' for its participants.[14] A decade later the same thing was being said by Bero Rigauer, a German social critic. According to Rigauer, 'the worker can no longer dispose of his skills.... his room for choice has been reduced to a minimum... The rational planning of athletic behaviour dominates ... goals are broken down into individual parts and phases, which are then carried out separately, or in small sequences.'[15] The critique was mild compared to the scathing derision of French political activist, Jean-Marie Brohm, who believed that the vocabulary of the machine had come to dominate the language of sport, and in doing so, comprehensively mechanised the athletic experience.[16] As a result, sport's value had been completely stripped away, with industrial capitalism to blame.

Sport's many challenges were also interrogated by Jessica Luther and Kavitha Davidson in their 2020 publication *Loving Sports When They Don't Love You Back: Dilemmas of the Modern Fan*. Luther and Davidson discussed these dilemmas under catchy headings which included: 'Rooting for your team when the star is accused of domestic violence'; 'Loving baseball despite its free market ideology'; 'Embracing tennis despite its inequities'; 'Watching football even when we know about brain trauma'; 'Cheering for a team with a racist mascot'; 'Forgiving the doper you love'; and 'Living with the new stadium you don't want.'[17]

When it comes to sport's commercialisation, there is still vigorous disagreement on what it contributes to the sporting experience of players and fans. In a recent study on the response of fans to sport's commercial growth, the findings revealed a lot of fan ambivalence. On one hand, fans appreciated the vast improvements in stadia design and comfort, but they were also concerned with the 'Disneyfication' of the game, with nearly everything that moved being branded, the relentless 'Celebritisation' of players, and the consequent undermining of 'team authenticity.'[18]

The Contradictions of Sport

It seemed that the deeper we dug into sporting structures and experiences, the more ambiguous it all became. For every study that confirmed sport's ability to enhance the well-being of citizens, there were several others that pointed to a social problem it had exacerbated. Moreover, rank-and-file citizens could not agree on sport's institutional status, which was highlighted in a 2021 study of just over 1,000 Belgian sport followers conducted by Jens De Rycke and Veerle De Bosscher.[19] The results were fascinating, mainly because they showed a strong division of opinion amongst respondents.

Some of the findings placed sport in a very positive light. For example, while 15% of respondents totally believed that elite sport promoted the separation of people with different religions, cultures, and origins, 58% totally believed that elite sport promoted the integration of people with different religions, cultures, and ethnic origins. But other findings from the study were not quite as effusive. For example, while 15% of respondents indicated that elite sport assisted people to withdraw from a gambling addiction, 38% thought that elite sport engagement was a pathway to addiction.[20]

Facing the Ambiguities

We find ourselves mired in sport's often-mysterious role in capturing the hearts and minds of millions of people across the planet despite its sometimes-violent underbelly. In the following chapter, we aim to better understand sport's unique capability to make a difference, as well as its transformative possibilities. At the same time, it highlights the ways in which things can go horribly wrong, where societal capital is stripped away, large slabs of public value are destroyed, and people are harmed. But throughout the journey, our minds will be focused on not only what sport currently does well or badly but also on how it can be improved and its value maximised, all in the name of citizen well-being. In short, we want to see if sport can deliver on its promises and, in doing so, make society a better place.

Notes

1 Richard Bailey (2005). Evaluating the relationship between physical education, sport and social inclusion, *Educational Review*, 57 (1): 71–90.
2 Maurico Marques, Luciano Alencastro, and Rodrigo de Vargas (2017). Youth positive development through sport: Strategies from social project coaches in Brazil and Spain, in Dell'Aglio, D. and Koller, S. (eds) *Vulnerable Children and Youth in Brazil,* Springer: 129–139.
3 Jim Parry (2012). The power of sport in peacemaking and peacekeeping, *Sport in Society*, Online publication.
4 Laura Zanotti, Max Stephenson, and Marcy Schnitzer (2015). Biopolitical and disciplinary peacebuilding: Sport, reforming bodies and rebuilding societies, *International Peacekeeping*, 22 (2): 186–201.
5 Jeeyoon Kim and David Jeffrey (2019). Sport and happiness: Understanding the relations among sport consumption activities, long-and short-term subjective well-being, and psychological need fulfilment, *Journal of Sport Management*, 33 (2): 119–132.
6 An excellent primer on the problems faced by sport as the 2010s unfolded – especially in the USA – was Dave Zirin (2013). *Game Over: How Politics Has Turned the Sports World Upside Down, The New Press.* Zirin not only provided a savage critique of the hyper-commercialisation of contemporary sport but also explained how, in recent times, as sport took on an array of social causes, it had paradoxically – and in his mind, thankfully – become a mouthpiece for protecting the vulnerable, the disadvantaged, and those facing the prospect of harm.

7 Eric Anderson and Adam White (2018). *Sport, Theory and Social Problems: A Critical Introduction*, Routledge.
8 Jay Coakley (2021) *Sport in Society. Issues & Controversies*, McGraw Hill.
9 David Andrews (2019). *Making Sport Great Again: The Uber-Sport Assemblage, Neoliberalism, and the Trump Conjuncture*, Palgrave Macmillan.
10 David Andrews (2019). *Making Sport Great Again*: 6–11.
11 David Andrews (2019). *Making Sport Great Again:* 16–18.
12 David Andrews (2019). *Making Sport Great Again*: 154–155.
13 Munene Mwaniki (2023). The case for Marxist–Leninist sport: Going beyond the limitations of western liberalism, *Sociology of Sport Journal*, 40 (4): 441–451.
14 Harry Edwards (1973). *The Sociology of Sport*, Dorsey Press.
15 Bero Rigauer (1981). *Sport and Work*, Columbia University Press: 30–32.
16 Jean-Marie Brohm (1978). *Sport: A Prison of Measured Time*, Ink Links: 29.
17 Jessica Luther and Kavitha Davidson (2020). *Loving Sports When They Don't Love You Back: Dilemmas of the Modern Fan*, University of Texas Press.
18 These and many other issues were examined in Erik Winell, John Armbrecht, Erik Lundberg and Jonas Nilsson (2023). How are fans affected by the commercialization of elite sports? A review of the literature and a research agenda, *Sport, Business and Management: An International Journal*, 13 (1): 118–137.
19 Jens De Rycke and Veerle De Bosscher (2021). The cure or the cause? Public opinions of elite sports' societal benefits and harms, *Sport in Society*, 24 (7): 1070–1092.
20 The results for each of the 79 items are listed in pp. 1078–1080.

4 Conceptual Constructs Revisited

Social Utility

In Chapter 1, we signalled our intention to frame our study around the notions of public value (PV) and the accumulation of capital, while also referring to the related concepts of social utility and the common good. But before we get into the analysis, we thought it would be helpful to begin with a brief discussion of social utility. Social utility has its foundations in the 19th-century utilitarian theories of Jeremy Bentham and John Stuart Mill,[1] who posited that any activity that delivered more benefits than harms was worth supporting, since it would enhance the overall happiness of a community. It gained an influential place in economics with the publication of Arthur Pigou's *The Economics of Welfare* in 1920 and quickly became an umbrella term covering the usefulness, satisfaction, or enjoyment consumers could secure from a service or good. It was informed by rational choice theory, which assumed that consumers would seek out experiences that increased utility while avoiding actions that lowered it. In short, social utility became a reference point for improving the welfare of society by focusing on the health, happiness, and financial well-being of people. As Pigou noted early in *The Economics of Welfare*, the 'main motive of economic study is to help social improvement.'[2]

While utility was 'real,' it was also understood as being notoriously difficult to quantify. That has not stopped it from being used as a guide to action in the field of public health, where doing the greatest good for the greatest number has become an embedded axiom.[3] It has also been applied to the world of sport, where policies, regulations, and rules are frequently used to enhance the utility, pleasure, and happiness of participants and spectators alike.[4] These themes were examined by Robert Schneider in his 2010 paper on *Developing Moral Sport Policies.* Schneider concluded that the 19th-century writings of Bentham and Mill and the 20th-century analysis by Pigou had a lot to offer sport managers in the 21st century.[5] Schneider's work was adapted by Harri Jalonen and his colleagues in their 2018 study into the utility – or customer 'value,' as they called it – of sport products.[6] Having examined the value creation process arising from the

DOI: 10.4324/9781003546931-4

nexus between sport and business, they identified five forms of value creation, all of which had relevance to people's engagement with sport, be it as players or fans. They were functional value (the product's usefulness), social value (the kudos and status it delivers), emotional value (the product's ability to elicit strong feeling), epistemic value (the product's capacity to arouse curiosity and a need to know more), and conditional value (the ability of a product to aid in the completion of a clearly defined task). Jalonen and his colleagues decided that the value creation process in sport entailed an eclectic mix of factors that went well beyond functionality and economic benefit, with emotional and symbolical value mostly underpinning the experience.

Public Value

The PV concept came out of studies into public administration where it addressed the citizen and community benefits – or well-being – that followed from the delivery of public services and related products. In local government circles especially, service quality varied enormously, where limited resources and vague promises were recipes for disappointing outcomes.[7] PV was given international currency with the publication of Mark Moore's groundbreaking work, *Creating Public Value: Strategic Management in Government*, in 1995.[8] According to Moore, everything could be explained by viewing the service delivery process as a 'strategic triangle.' He argued that PV would be optimised when (1) the legitimising authority – which was in effect the surrounding community, (2) the operational and administrative capabilities of the provider, and (3) the values, goals, and mission driving the initiative – the provider's value proposition, if you like – were perfectly aligned. Satisfying the strategic triangle would provide a net benefit to society.[9]

To put it another way, service providers would deliver optimal levels of PV – and thus enhance citizen well-being – if they met three conditions. First, the provider's service had secured community endorsement as a legitimate use of public funds; second, the provider's resource base was sufficient to deliver on their service promise; and finally, the provider had the management know-how to deliver the service efficiently.[10] Further, when it came to measuring PV, it was best left in the hands of citizens – the beneficiaries – who were best positioned to decide on service quality, value for money, and the extent to which a social problem was avoided, diminished, or exacerbated.[11]

While a multitude of studies have been undertaken into sport's capacity to attract participants and provide pathways to elite-level competitions, only a few have gone the extra step and examined its ability to build PV and enhance the well-being and quality of life of citizens, especially when it comes to security, safety, public health, personal growth, social cohesion, inclusion, prosperity, and happiness.

In 2009, Stephen Brookes and Jay Wiggan wrote a pioneering article on the application of PV concepts to the world of sport, *'Reflecting the Public Value of Sport: A Game of Two Halves?'*[12] Having consulted with sporting administrators, bureaucrats, and players, Brookes and Wiggan concluded that PV creation in sport was all about 'adding value to the social, physical and economic well-being of communities and individuals.'[13] This was the endgame, so to speak. The means of getting there were multi-faceted but generally came down to opening-up participation to all, supporting sporting excellence, helping to build healthy and happy communities, and doing it all in a cost-effective way.

PV creation was also the focus of a 2021 study we cited in the previous chapter. It was Willem der Roest and Bake Dijk's research paper, '*Developing an Elite Sports' Public Value Proposition in Northern Netherlands,*'[14] which sought to identify the conditions needed to legitimise PV propositions around investments in the elite end of sport development. der Roest and Dijk directed their attention to infrastructure, coaching, and conditioning programmes; the scheduling of competitions; and ancillary staffing arrangements. They hypothesised that support from government, the corporate sector, and the broader community for a PV proposition (side 1 of Moore's strategic triangle) would be strongest where the evidence for the anticipated 'pay-off' – that is, enhanced PV – was most convincing. But de Roest and Dijk cautioned readers that 'evidence' could come in various guises, with emotive appeal, intuitive understanding, and personal judgement at one end of the spectrum, and methodologically sound empirical research at the other.

Capital-Building Capability

The concept of capital had its origins in the world of business during the Middle Ages when any money loaned to a merchant or entrepreneur was viewed as an income-yielding asset to the lender. By the time the industrial revolution had come along, it was commonly understood as the funds invested in a business-related enterprise. By the middle of the 20th century, the concept of capital had been bifurcated into physical and human, with Theodore Schultz – an American economist – using it to reflect the 'value of human capacities.' During the 1980s it was re-fashioned by Amartya Sen – an economist at Harvard University in the USA – as a measure of 'human capabilities.' In Sen's mind, if a person has the freedom to make choices around education, health, and building a career, they will not only achieve more but also add to the quality of life of others. In making this claim, Sen acknowledged the influence of Adam Smith, the 18th-century political economist, who argued that education, learning, and a supportive social environment could transform people's lives.[15] In the 1990s, sociologists ran with the concept, Pierre Bourdieu leading the way.[16] He introduced the ideas of economic, social, cultural, and symbolic capital and used them to reveal class and status differences within society.[17] Over the past two decades, these concepts have underpinned research projects looking at sport's capacity to enhance participants' material status, physical health, psychological well-being, and social connectedness, and thus improve societal well-being.[18]

In addressing the social utility, PV, and capital-building capability of sport, we acknowledge the challenges. It is one thing to identify a situation where, for example, PV has been enhanced by increased participation levels in disadvantaged communities or by a major event that captured the public's imagination, but it is another thing to assign it a monetary figure. The same problem emerges when having to deal with situations where PV has been diminished due to a costly infrastructure failure or drug-use scandal. Yet, on the positive side of the sport development ledger, a vast amount of research has been undertaken in recent times on the role sport plays in contemporary society and the impact it delivers. This issue will be examined further in the following chapter.

Notes

1 Jeremy Bentham and John Stuart Mill (2004). *Utilitarianism and Other Essays*, Penguin.

2 Arthur Pigou (1920). *The Economics of Welfare*, Macmillan and Co. Limited.

3 See, for example, Kathryn MacKay (2017). Perspectives: Utility and justice in public health, *Journal of Public Health*, 40 (3): 413–418; and Julian Savulescu, Ingmar Persson and Dominic Wilkinson (2020). Utilitarianism and the pandemic, *Bioethics*, 34: 620–632.

4 For a recent application of social utility theory to the world of sport and recreation, see B. Liu, Y. Chen, and M. Xiao (2020). The social utility and health benefits for older adults of amenity buildings in China's urban parks: A Nanjing case study, *International Journal of Environmental Research and Public Health,* 17 (20): Online publication.

5 Robert Schneider (2010). Developing moral sport policies through act-utilitarianism based on Bentham's hedonic calculus, *Sport Management International Journal*, 6 (2): Online publication.

6 Harri Jalonen, Sasu Tuominen, Arto Ryömä, Jaakko Haltia, Juho Nenonen, and Anna Kuikka (2018). How does value creation manifest itself in the nexus of sport and business? A systematic literature review, *Open Journal of Business and Management*, 6: 103–113.

7 For a contemporary example, see Graham Atkins and Stuart Hoddinott (2022). *Neighbourhood Services under Strain: How a Decade of Cuts and Rising Demand for Social Care Affected Local Services*, Institute for Government UK.

8 Mark Moore (1995). *Creating Public Value: Strategic Management in Government*, Harvard University Press.

9 For an update on the subsequent application and significance of Moore's 'strategic triangle,' see Timo Meynhardt (2009). Public value inside: What is public value creation? *International Journal of Public Administration*, 32 (3): 192–219; Nicholas Faulkner and Stefan Kaufman (2018). Avoiding theoretical stagnation: A systematic review and framework for measuring public value, *Australian Journal of Public Administration*, 77 (1): 69–86; and Janine O'Flynn (2021). Where to for public value?

Taking stock and moving on, *International Journal of Public Administration*, 44 (10): 867–877.

10 Janine O'Flynn (2007). From new public management to public value: Paradigmatic change and managerial implications, *Australian Journal of Public Administration*, 66 (3): 353–366.

11 O'Flynn (2007). From new public management to public value.

12 Stephen Brookes and Jay Wiggan (2009). Reflecting the public value of sport: A game of two halves? *Public Management Review*, 11 (4): 401–420.

13 Stephen Brookes and Jay Wiggan (2009). *Reflecting the Public Value of Sport*: 415.

14 Willem der Roest and Bake Dijk (2021). Developing an elite sports' public value proposition in Northern Netherlands, *European Sport Management Quarterly*, 21 (5): 677–694.

15 For more details in the human capabilities approach to capital building, see Baldwin Ranson (1987). The Institutionalist theory of capital formation, *Journal of Economic Issues*, 21 (3): 1265–1278; Amartya Sen (1987). Editorial - Human capital and human capability, *World Development*, 25 (12): Online publication; and Martha Nussbaum (2011). *Creating Capabilities: The Human Development Approach*, Belknap Press.

16 Pierre Bourdieu (1986). The forms of capital. In: John G. Richardson (ed.): *Handbook of Theory and Research for the Sociology of Education*, Greenwood Press: 241–258.

17 For an excellent arm-length analysis of Bourdieu's models of capital accumulation and social advancement, see Xiaowei Huang (2019). Understanding Bourdieu - Cultural capital and habitus, *Review of European Studies*, 11 (3): 45–49.

18 See, for example, Ran Zhou and Kiki Kaplanidou (2017). Building social capital from sport event participation: An exploration of the social impacts of participatory sport events on the community, *Sport Management Review*, 21 (5): 491-503: and Yi-Hsiu Lin (2022). Antecedents and outcomes of social capital: Evidence from a professional baseball franchise, *Psychology Research and Behavior Management*, 15: 261–272.

5 The Public Value of Sport

As we indicated in Chapter 2, sport goes well beyond the real-time and deep-seated pleasure it gives its participants. It has been given the role of making society a better place by transforming its followers into better people and more engaged citizens. But is it all too good to be true? People who believe sport can change society for the better have come up with many examples of how it works and the benefits that follow.[1] Many of the claims were intrinsically sensible, but we also had the uneasy feeling that some went beyond the probable and moved into the world of the grandiosely unprovable.

Let's start by summarising them one by one to address the associated propositions and generalise to what extent they have been shown to deliver on their public value promises. In keeping with the sport policy work done by Willem der Roest and Bake Dijk in the Netherlands, we decided to call them public value propositions, or PVP for short. De Roest and Djik argued that PVPs were important instruments for legitimising government spending on sporting infrastructure, related programmes, and consequent staffing arrangements. This is because the stronger the value proposition, the greater the likelihood that key stakeholders (local communities, the media, the corporate sector, governments, and the like) will give their support. De Roest and Dijk also noted that since the social and economic impacts – and by implication, PVPs – will differ from sport to sport and place to place, the level of funding for their development will reflect these differences.

We got down to business by breaking up the myths and beliefs surrounding sport into bite-sized chunks. We subsequently created 15 PVPs, which are listed as follows:

1 Sport makes people smarter and more knowledgeable.
2 Sport builds character by turning callow youths into responsible and civic-minded adults.
3 Sport makes its participants morally virtuous by having them deal with conflicted choices.
4 Sport participants have more friends than those who did not engage with sport.

DOI: 10.4324/9781003546931-5

5 The sporting achievements of elite athletes create positive role models for emulation by young people.
6 Sport engagement lowers the incidence of juvenile crime by giving young people something to aspire to.
7 Sport participation makes people happy by fulfilling grand ambitions and heroic dreams.
8 Sport enables people to live healthier and longer lives with fewer disabilities.
9 Sport engagement protects participants from long-term psychological harm.
10 Sport is a safety valve for the release of pent-up aggression and hostility.
11 Sport enables its participants to build work-ready capabilities that result in high-wage jobs.
12 Sport contributes to the growth of local economies by attracting infrastructure, visitor expenditure, and more jobs.
13 Sport is an ideal site for promoting social causes and changing social behaviour.
14 Sport provides places for fans to become active members of intimately engaged communities.
15 Sport provides safe and protective spaces for securing exhilarating experiences.

We recognise that our selection of 15 PVPs might seem arbitrary, but our selection was based on careful analysis of the claims made about sport's ability to make society a better place. Since this book is just a 'primer,' we encourage interested readers to consult our lengthier treatise on the subject for a more detailed explanation of not only our rationale for the choice of 15 PVPs and their formulation but also how we went about synthesising our empirical studies.[2] Next we unpacked each PVP. We've also provided salient research citations in the endnotes which will enable readers to secure source documents with a minimum of fuss.

Public Value Propositions

PVP 1: Sport makes people smarter and more knowledgeable

The research studies assembled under this heading suggested that not only did sport participation do little harm to the intellectual development of children and adolescents, but in many instances led to a significant improvement in school grades. Yet this applied mostly to boys. The studies we examined also showed that when it came to the scholastic benefits from sport engagement, diminishing returns clicked in early in the process. That is, most of the benefits came with the initial exposure. So, if you wanted your already sporty child to succeed academically, then the best course of action was to give them more academic instruction, not more sports education. As John Phillips and Walter Schafer[3] noted in their early classic studies, sport did not directly contribute to high grades but rather provided the disciplinary framework for prioritising classroom learning. In other words, there were times in everyone's lives – especially in adolescence – where a bit of sport was more than enough. So, sport does not, of itself, make you smarter, but neither does it stifle academic learning and intellectual development. To round things off, there was additional evidence which suggested that play (which is, as we now know, a rudimentary precursor of sport, but keeps the spontaneity intact) can improve the learning capabilities of children when embedded in the curricula.[4]

PVP 2: Sport builds character by turning callow youths into responsible and civic-minded adults

Despite studies which showed that not all sports had character-building properties, it would be imprudent to think that sport had no positive impact on the disposition and social capabilities of young people. Diann Eley and David Kirk's[5] 2002 study showed that sport could enhance young people's civic engagement, while the 2012 study by Carreres Ponsoda and her colleagues[6] also revealed positive personal and social outcomes. The same went for the 2017 study conducted by Alfonso Valero Valenzuela and his colleagues.[7] Despite the limitations of the reviews by Nicholas Holt and his colleagues[8] in 2017, and Christiana Bessa and her colleagues[9] in 2019, they revealed many instances where opportunities for character building occurred. But it also appeared that certain conditions had to be in place to ensure a beneficial sporting experience and not have it degenerate into a chaotic free-for-all. Sport delivered on its character-building promises only when it was part of a programme that was well organised, had a caring ethos, had eliminated the likelihood of serious harms occurring, and was staffed by properly trained administrators, officials, coaches, and relevant support personnel. Playing sport in a club-based setting where winning was the main aim was a hit-and-miss affair when it came to building character.[10]

PVP 3: Sport embeds its participants with a strong sense of morality

For about 150 years, we were led to believe that the best education you could get when it came to the moral development of young men and, more lately, women was to immerse them in a sporting enterprise that focused on rough-and-tumble team games. This is where lifelong lessons were learnt about the difference between right and wrong, and fair and unfair, not to mention all the learnings that accompany winning and losing. In short, doing sport made its participants morally virtuous. When you look at the evidence, however, the opposite was the case. Sport's capacity for inculcating its participants with a strong ethical framework was modest, while its potential to inflict harm was considerable. There were many instances where violence, cheating, and insidious gameplay had destroyed the integrity of sport and squeezed all the fun and exhilaration out of it for nearly everybody. To put it in more theoretical language, the research said that moral reasoning regressed to a more selfish stage of moral development in sport compared to everyday life. This is in line with 'bracketed morality theory,' which posited that moral reasoning was moderated by the context in which moral dilemmas were being addressed. Thus, it should come as no surprise to find that sport – especially where competition is high – will teach young people that stretching the rules to gain an advantage is just part of the game.[11] Sport was also shown in studies to be problematic where harms to others were exacerbated, and fair play was sidelined. The studies by Brenda Jo Bredemeier and David Shields[12] showed disintegration of participants' attitudes and behaviours when winning became the primary objective.

PVP 4: Sport participants have more friends than those who did not engage with sport

When it came to finding out if sport engagement strengthened interpersonal relationships and built social capital, the evidence was indisputable. It did.[13] This was not surprising since sport is, by its very nature, a social experience. As we noted in earlier chapters, sport was only possible when an opponent turned up. If you wanted to play alone, then Solitaire was perfect. Sport, however, demanded interaction with real people in real time. Moreover, sport involved organisation where clubs were front and centre, and being a team member was always a likely prospect. But the evidence also demonstrated that the capacity for sport to establish friendships was not evenly distributed either between or within clubs and teams. Team sports generated more friendships than individual sports, while taking on administrative responsibilities did the same. What's more, bonding social capital tended to be the dominant outcome whether the teams were homogenised or diverse. A gregarious personality provided a social advantage, but building friendships was challenging for introverts, those with a preference for individual sports, and those whose sporting skills had not fully matured. In these instances, social invisibility was the more likely outcome. Overall, we found that sport was a significant contributor to friendship building, especially for young people.[14] In addition, the network of friends developed through sport often provided the social support for engaging in other sporting and social activities as well.[15]

PVP 5: The sporting achievements of elite athletes create positive role models for emulation by young people

So, what can we say about sport's ability to utilise elite athlete success – and their frequent elevation to hero status – to get more young people playing sport and building lifestyles around health, fitness, and pro-social behaviour? For the most part, the findings indicated that the above belief has been based on myth more than fact. Role modelling was far less influential in getting young people to be fitter,[16] healthier, more engaged in community activities, and more socially aware than has been previously supposed.[17] There was even less evidence to suggest that role models from the world of sport had changed the beliefs and attitudes of young people. It made intuitive sense that superstar athletes would be the perfect people for disseminating messages of inspiration and hope to the world's youth. Unfortunately, the idea that elite sports men and women had the power to shape the behaviour of young people in positive ways had little evidence to back it up. While sporting role models were, in the short term, taken notice of, that was mostly where it ended. But this has not stopped many sport officials, media commentators, and politicians from arguing that elite athletes – especially those with a strong media presence – have an obligation to do the right thing and grasp their role modelling opportunities.[18] Notwithstanding this inspirational challenge, we were forced to conclude that sport's capacity to create influential role models had been seriously over-rated, while the 'trickle-down effect' was largely based on wishful thinking rather than evidence.[19]

PVP 6: Sport engagement lowers the incidence of juvenile crime by giving young people something to aspire to

This claim has had great appeal to many of sport's stakeholders for a long time. There was a taken-for-granted belief in sport's ability to reduce violence, promote pro-social behaviour, and control aggression and juvenile delinquency. Unfortunately, the studies we explored concluded that sport's ability to keep wayward youth on the straight and narrow could not be guaranteed. Whereas the 2006 USA study into midnight basketball programmes conducted by Douglas Hartmann and Brooks Depro[20] found incidents where inner-city crime rates fell, the 2009 study into American adolescent deviant behaviour by Margot Gardner, Jodie Roth, and Jeanne Brooks-Gunn,[21] drew a blank. The dominant influences on juvenile crime have always been unemployment, a lack of education, poverty, and peer group pressure. When weighed up against these factors, even the best-run and resourced sport-related interventions where participants reported major improvements in self-esteem, personal confidence, and sociability were not always able to reverse their delinquent and/or criminal tendencies.[22] To conclude, sport was no panacea for alleviating delinquency or reducing criminal activity, but, on balance, sport-based interventions to get at-risk teenagers back on the path to normality have delivered more happiness than harm.[23]

PVP 7: Sport participation makes people happy by fulfilling grand ambitions and heroic dreams

On balance, sport engagement made people happier than they would have been had they not involved themselves in some type of sporting activity, although it's possible that a lot of this has to do with physical activity and social connections.[24] The only dispute was around the scale and duration of the feelings of happiness. Some studies suggested that the happiness gains were slight and little different from the benefits accrued from other leisure pursuits and hobbies like eating out, adventure travel, cabinet making, needlework, arts and crafts, embracing an organised religion, and doing volunteer work for disadvantaged communities.[25] Nor was there a lot of evidence to support the claim that the relationship between sport participation and happiness was long lasting.[26] Happiness was often intense but fleeting.[27] As many studies have shown, happiness can be severely undermined by declining health, a loss of a partner, or an abusive marriage. Loving, stable relationships, on the other hand, made people happy for long periods of time, with sport participation being just one of many pathways to happiness. As the 2011 study by Tim Pawlowski, Paul Downward, and Simona Rasciute[28] showed, it was a journey worth taking. At the same time, there was no guarantee that unhappy people could simply turn their feelings around by spending more time on the sporting field and less time trawling the internet.

PVP 8: Sport enables people to live healthier and longer lives with fewer disabilities

While the studies we examined generally reinforced anecdotal, non-expert observations that sport participation had a positive effect on health and longevity, they did note some negative behaviours as well.[29] These were succinctly documented in the 2010 study conducted by Lindsay Taliaferro, Barbara Rienzo, and Kristine Donovan, which examined the relationships between sport participation and health risk behaviours amongst American high school students.[30] Team sport participants were more likely to use smokeless tobacco and binge drink than non-participants. Sport participants also had a higher risk of disordered eating. We were not prepared to say that sport's capacity to build healthy communities was over-rated. This went against the considered pronouncements of nearly every health professional around the world. We were on safer ground, though, when we softened our position by reminding ourselves that people would be better off in all sorts of ways by being physically active, with sport being a powerful tool for making it happen in a highly socialised, if sometimes intimidating, setting.[31] When it came to identifying those sports which delivered a longer life, there was no consensus, although one UK study found that tennis, swimming, and aerobic programmes were particularly impactful.[32]

PVP 9: Sport engagement protects participants from long-term psychological harm by alleviating anxiety, stress, and depression

This PVP contained enough evidence to support claims that sport engagement had the potential to protect its participants – especially young adults – from psychological harm. There were also data to show that if children and adolescents were exposed to well-administered sports programmes, the greater their chance of growing up into relatively well-adjusted adults who could manage stress, exhibit some degree of psychological resilience, suffer fewer bouts of depression, and enjoy frequent moments of 'life satisfaction.' The 2019 study by Molly Easterlin and her colleagues found that team sports participation, especially, had made a significant contribution to the psychological health of young Americans exposed to adverse childhood experiences.[33] A couple of other studies found that sport was often enjoyed for its own sake when participants were 'in the moment,' so to speak. In these instances, it engendered intense happiness. This intrinsic benefit should never be underestimated. There were also moments when participants reported reduced anxiety and stress levels when just being physically active.[34] In some instances – where sport created its own pressures – anxiety levels increased.[35] But overall, sport and its associated physical activity, had a unique capacity to protect young people from many mental health conditions.[36]

PVP 10: Sport – especially at the highly competitive level – is a safety valve for the release of stress and pent-up aggression

The studies we examined showed, first and foremost, that playing sport at the highly competitive level was a stressful experience.[37] What's more, these stresses were sometimes associated with various forms of psychological disorders, with anxiety and depression prominent. They confirmed anecdotal stories about professional athletes who often sought refuge from the pressures they faced by removing themselves from the public gaze and seeking professional support.[38] We can also safely say that people who played individual sports were less likely to enjoy their sporting experiences and more likely to exhibit anxiety and suffer from depression than those who engaged in team sports. As it turned out, three of the most common influences were injury, overtraining, and burnout.[39] The other lesson we took away from these studies is that sport was not a social safety valve where pent-up anger and aggressive feelings could be dissipated on the playing field. If anything, the studies showed that the pressures to be aggressive on the field of play often leaked into off-field settings. One 2011 study conducted by Pippa Grange and John Kerr provided solid evidence that amongst elite players, aggression and violence frequently strayed from the playing field into the social world.[40] This phenomenon was also spotted in elite youth sports programmes.[41]

PVP 11: Sport in school enables its participants to build work-ready capabilities that result in high-wage jobs with prospects for advancement

Some evidence has demonstrated that sport participation at high school and university appeared to give participants a head-start when it came to making a good living in the adult phase of their lives. The 2003 study conducted by James Curtis, William McTeer, and Philip White[42] into the workplace earnings for Canadian student-athletes provided unconditional confirmation, as did the 2009 German study conducted by Michael Lechner.[43] However, these studies lead to the question of how, exactly, sport participation was associated with higher workforce earnings. For example, are sport people more intelligent, are they more studious, are they more socially adept, are they more ambitious, and are they more comfortable fitting in with the demands of organisational life? Or are they just more healthy and more energetic? Alternatively, are they more committed to becoming successful and letting others know about it?

There seems to be an element of truth in most of these factors, but the relative strength of each factor is still not known. At this point in time, we do not seem to have many precise answers on just how sport participation delivers, on average, a fatter pay cheque to those who played sport during adolescence and early adulthood.[44] The results make it hard to dispute the fact that for someone intent on maximising their workplace earnings, doing sport at school and university was a good first step. So, yes, playing sport in school made its participants richer in later life, with no reason to think they would gravitate to low-wage jobs with poor prospects for advancement.[45] But at the same time, it remained plausible that the critical driver of that greater earnings potential was primarily the social networks accumulated during sporting participation rather than the actual sport activity itself.[46]

PVP 12: Sport contributes to the growth of local economies by attracting additional infrastructure, more visitor expenditure, and more jobs

It was often said that sport punched above its weight, which meant that its contribution to society was usually greater than you would expect given the limited resources it had at its disposal. However, the evidence we have provided so far suggests the claim is heavily over-optimistic. Neither should we get excited when it comes to the contribution sport has made to local, regional, and national economies. Professional sports teams and stadiums had 'very limited economic impacts,' and that 'even with added non-pecuniary social benefits from quality-of-life externalities and civic pride, the welfare improvements from hosting teams [fell] well short of covering public outlays.'[47] When government funding and in-kind support was accounted for, the net economic impact of sport events, clubs, and teams could be frighteningly low. In short, our analysis shows that whenever economic impact studies identified only the benefit side of the ledger, only half the story had been told.[48] Studies of this type only had legitimacy when they addressed the cost side of the ledger, where both capital and recurrent costs were part of the calculations.[49] When this was undertaken, the return-on-investment figures were often disappointingly low.[50] But it was also clear that investment in sport was a useful tool for renewing old inner-city districts. The UK research done by Larissa Davies[51] into sporting infrastructure in Sheffield and Cardiff suggested that the benefits to the local economy were solid.

PVP 13: Sport – because of its media-friendly image and broad public reach – is an ideal site for promoting social causes and changing social behaviour, especially when it addresses misogyny, homophobia, and racism

When taken in the context of pronouncements from sporting authorities and event promoters, it seemed as though the sporting world was leading the way when it came to social justice issues.[52] In the lead-in to the 2022 FIFA World Cup, Hassan al-Thawadi, the chief of Qatar's organising committee, got caught up in the euphoria when he reported that labour reforms achieved by Qatar had been 'historical' and the event would leave 'truly transformational social, cultural, economic and environmental legacies.'[53]

Unfortunately, the cases we reviewed told us something quite different about the day-to-day conduct of fans, players, and administrators. Fan optimism about how sport had changed social attitudes for the better was unfounded in most instances. They seemed to think that racism had been eradicated from the world of sport and that homophobia was on the cusp of being eliminated. However, our review documented the ongoing presence of both forms of discrimination, with misogyny and sexism lurking at every corner.[54] Brigid McCarthy's[55] 2022 research into skateboarding, together with Sarah Barnes and Mary Louise Adams'[56] work on the world of female coaches, suggested that sexist attitudes and misogynistic behaviour had worsened during the 2010s. As it also turned out, the media was a hotbed of gender discrimination, where, in the United States, in the early 2020s, less than 10% of all sport reporting was done by women.[57] Social media was worse and heading in the wrong direction.[58]

PVP 14: Sport provides places for fans to become active members of intimately engaged communities that engender meaning, a positive identity, and civic engagement

As we noted earlier, sport could be enjoyed in all sorts of ways, one of which was being a fan. It provided a common talking point with friends, and it delivered a strong sense of community. It also got people excited and built an identity. A 2016 UK study on football fans by John Obinna Onwe,[59] and the 2021 USA study by Elizabeth Delia, Jeffrey James, and Daniel Wann[60] into sport fandom, confirmed that fans' close connection to their teams not only gave their lives meaning, but also gave them a reason to get out of bed in the morning. There were also a few downsides. The excitement (or eustress, as it is sometimes called) could quickly turn into violence, especially when alcohol was nearby.[61] More worryingly, it seemed that too much emotion amongst older men increased the risk of succumbing to some form of heart disease, or even heart failure.[62] It further appeared that sport fandom had become addictive in some instances, where the psychological hit that accompanied a close game that ended in victory became etched in the brain.[63] Finally, while sport fandom could make people feel good about themselves and the world around them, it could also be fleeting and pass without trace.[64] But it was hard to ignore the fact that millions of fans have reported feeling good about themselves and their place in the world when their team did well.[65] So, in summary, sport fandom can be deliriously joyful but often comes with significant costs.[66]

PVP 15: Sport provides safe spaces for securing exhilarating experiences

American social commentator Michael Novak claimed that playing sports gave a glimpse of eternity, 'a foretaste of the eschaton' (the death and destiny of mankind), and an opportunity to 'break the ordinary bonds of mortality.'[67] But sport will not always deliver ecstatic experiences. It can also be prosaic and even dysfunctional. This alternative reality was captured by Toben Nelson and Harold Wechsler, who examined heavy episodic alcohol consumption amongst USA college students.[68] Their 1997 study showed that college student-athletes consumed a lot more alcohol than their non-sport counterparts. The situation got worse when we found that performance-enhancing drug use was still rampant, and despite the conscientious efforts of WADA, everything appeared to be spiralling out of control.[69] Illicit drug use was everywhere in sport, and binge drinking had not lost its appeal to young adults who liked to engage with sport. The extent to which sport participation encourages violence has been widely researched,[70] and books have been written about it.[71] Violence can be endemic and has great appeal for fans who have a deeply instinctive interest in 'blood being spilt.'[72]

As for gambling, the risk of physical injury was low, but the risk of incurring a psychological disorder was getting higher by the moment.[73] Even more startlingly, strong evidence emerged that communities had a massive injury cost to deal with, which would only get larger as more women played contact sports at the elite level, and the long-term impact of concussions was better understood. However, the worst was yet to come. A 2022 study conducted by the Australian government's health research and promotion agency found that when the health benefits of sport participation were balanced against the costs of securing them, the risks and associated costs outweighed the benefits by a wide margin. We were not surprised to hear in late 2022 that the Australian government had established a parliamentary committee to examine concussion and repeated head trauma in contact sport.[74] It came hot on the heels of a UK Parliament decision to examine the concussion in sport problem, having been shocked by research studies which found that soccer-football had an issue with players 'heading' the ball.[75] While it has been a fundamental game skill for more than a century, it is now no longer permitted at some junior levels.

In early 2023, sport's claim that it taught participants how to act ethically was once again blown out of the water when it was shown that cheating was endemic in the paralympic movement. An Australian television documentary revealed that many participants had exaggerated – and in some instances feigned – their disability to relocate to a category or classification that gave them a better chance of securing a top-three finish.[76] To make matters worse, a spate of match-fixing scandals have been exposed over the last decade or so, with cricket[77] and (soccer) football[78] in the thick of it.

We were forced to concede that sport had become a dangerous and sometimes corrupt enterprise where safe spaces could no longer be guaranteed.

Reflecting on the PVPs

There is also another way of looking at the above claims, and that is to view them through the lens of the sporting public.[79] As we briefly noted in Chapter 3, this is exactly what two Belgian researchers, Jens De Rycke and Veerle De Bosscher, did in 2021, when they conducted a study into how the public viewed the 'social societal benefits and harms' from sport participation. They directed their attention to elite sport rather than community sport because they wanted to find out how average Belgian taxpayers felt about the use of their money to fund an aspect of sport that focused on a few privileged players and athletes. We were especially interested in their findings since they would give us an indication of the extent to which the public's views and opinions about what sport can do for society replicate independent research findings.

De Rycke and De Bosscher were perfectly placed to do the research since they had just formulated a questionnaire to secure this type of data. It was based on the Mapping Elite Sport's Societal Impact (MESSI) framework. It was hugely expansive and included 79 items that related to the positive and negative societal impacts of elite sport.

The questionnaire invited people to respond to each item by having them state if they agreed with a claim or its opposite. For example, item 1 contained two opposing statements, one of which claimed that elite sport promoted the separation of people with different religions, cultures, and origins, with the other claiming that elite sport promoted the integration of people with different religions, cultures, and origins. Respondents had to decide which of the two statements most accurately represented their views. The questionnaire was completed by 1102 Belgian citizens.

As it turned out, 15% totally believed that elite sport promoted the separation of people with different religions, cultures, and origins, while 58% totally believed that elite sport promoted the integration of people with different religions, cultures, and origins. The remaining 37% were ambivalent. The results for item 15 were also quite illuminating. Whereas 21% totally agreed with the claim that elite sport encouraged cheating, 55% totally agreed with the counter claim that sport encouraged fair play. Item 41 examined the contentious issue of role modelling. While 15% of respondents totally believed that elite sport provided athletes only a minimal role model function, 68% of them totally believed that it provided athletes with a profound role modelling function.

The study provided many fascinating results, but not all of them were as effusive as the above findings might indicate. In fact, some findings hinted that elite sport also had a few challenges to deal with. For example, item 32 found that 15% of the public reckoned elite sport assisted people to withdraw from a gambling addiction. But 38% of the public thought that elite sport engagement was in fact a pathway to addiction. Item 45 also highlighted a problem with elite sport. While 45% of the public believed elite sport delivered its participants good health outcomes, a surprisingly high 39% believed it delivered serious health problems, with injuries and chronic stress being the major culprits.

Public concerns did not end there. When addressing item 48, 35% of the public thought elite sport promoted drug abuse amongst athletes. Only 30% thought it eliminated drug use amongst athletes. Item 70 also revealed concerns about elite sport doing good things. Whereas 27% of the public thought elite sport had a positive impact on the environment, 36% thought its impact was negative. Yet it was item 73 that elicited the most unfavourable finding. This item had to do with the number of local resources required to deliver a major sporting event when elite athletes were participating. At first glance, the responses were positive, with around 36% of the public believing the amount of local one-off costs incurred was justifiable. However, just over 42% of the public believed that these one-off costs were totally unjustified.[80]

Counting the Costs, Evaluating the Benefits, and Rating the Propositions

Having assembled the summaries reported under the 15 PVPs and having reflected on the study by De Rycke and De Bosscher, we felt confident we could rate each item. But we also found that there were three criteria to consider for each item.

The first related to each PVP's *mythological significance*. That is, to what extent were the PVPs an integral part of the culture of sport and defined its special qualities?

The second related to their match with *community and societal attitudes*. That is, did the public embrace each of the PVPs and see them as the essence of what was good about sport, or did they discard them as either unimportant or unachievable?

The third related to the *research evidence* that could be used to support the claims contained in the PVPs. Were the PVPs based on independent, high-quality research undertaken by experienced academics and policy analysts, or were they just good stories based in anecdote and wishful thinking?

Having decided upon the rating criteria, we then had to come up with a measuring stick for each one. For *mythological significance*, we estimated how much cultural weight sports officials, sports journalists, politicians, and policy advisors put on each PVP. We did this by re-visiting the research to see how often each PVP featured in the various government documents, sport-sponsored reports, and policy statements that were collated. When it came to gauging public sentiment through the lens of *community and societal attitudes,* we went directly to the research findings of De Rycke and De Bosscher in their 2021 paper, 'The cure or the cause?' In getting a feel for the *research evidence* that either supported or challenged each PVP, we returned to the mass of studies we evaluated to reach the conclusions summarised earlier.

If our findings met or exceeded the claims made for them, they were given a high rating, but if they did not meet the claims made for them, they were given a low rating. We ended up with the following Public Value Scorecard.

Table 5.1 provides some fascinating comparisons, where in some instances the research evidence is as high as you can get, but the mythical significance and community and societal attitude ratings are slight. But even more importantly, there are instances where the mythical significance and community and societal attitude rating are high but the research evidence demonstrated the PVP as unachievable, being based more in myth than fact.

With these revelations in mind, we assigned a score out of 10 for each PVP based on the weightings we gave for mythical significance, community and societal attitudes, and research evidence. We then located them in the 8–10 range (the PVP is highly achievable based on the research findings, while also having significant support from key stakeholders),

Table 5.1 Provisional Scores for Claims (PVPs) Made about Sport's Ability to Improve the Collective Well-Being of Citizens in Contemporary Society

#	*Nature of claim/Public value proposition*	*Mythical significance*	*Community and societal attitudes*	*Research evidence*
1	Sport makes people smarter and more knowledgeable.	Moderate	Low	Moderate
2	Sport builds character by turning callow youths into responsible and civic-minded adults	High	High	Moderate
3	Sport makes its participants morally virtuous by having them deal with conflicted choices	High	High	Minimal
4	Sport participants have more friends than those who did not engage with sport	High	High	High
5	The sporting achievements of elite athletes create positive role models for emulation by young people.	High	High	Low
6	Sport engagement lowers the incidence of juvenile crime by giving young people something to aspire to.	Medium	High	Moderate
7	Sport participation makes people happy by fulfilling grand ambitions and heroic dreams.	Moderate	Moderate	Moderate
8	Sport enables people to live healthier and longer lives with fewer disabilities.	High	High	Moderate
9	Sport engagement protects participants from long-term psychological harm.	Moderate	Moderate	Moderate
10	Sport is a safety valve for the release of pent-up aggression and hostility.	Moderate	High	Low
11	Sport enables its participants to build work-ready capabilities that result in high-wage jobs.	Low	Low	High
12	Sport contributes to the growth of local economies by attracting infrastructure, visitor expenditure, and more jobs.	High	High	Moderate
13	Sport is an ideal site for promoting social causes and changing social behaviour.	Low	Moderate	Low
14	Sport provides places for fans to become positively active members of intimately engaged communities.	Moderate	High	Moderate
15	Sport provides safe and protective spaces for securing exhilarating experiences.	High	Moderate	Low

the 5–7 range (the PVP is problematic, but with a groundswell of support could deliver on some of its promises), and the 0–4 range (the PVP is severely flawed and probably unachievable, while also lacking any useful support from key stakeholders). We ended up with the following 'credibility rating' in Table 5.2.

If this approach does not appeal all that much because of its numerical rigidity, then the following diagram in Table 5.3 may be a preferable way of categorising the findings. It not only provided a bit more flexibility by enabling some re-positioning to occur but also revealed the similarities and differences between the PVPs.

Table 5.2 Credibility ratings for PVPs

Rank	*Nature of claim/public value proposition*	*Credibility rating/score (0–10)*
1	Sport participants have more friends than those who did not engage with sport.	**10**
2	Sport enables people to live healthier and longer lives with fewer disabilities.	**9**
3	Sport protects youth and young adult participants from long-term psychological harm.	**8**
4	Sport makes people smarter and more knowledgeable.	**8**
5	Sport contributes to the growth of local economies by attracting infrastructure, visitor expenditure, and more jobs.	**8**
6	Sport participation makes people happy by fulfilling grand ambitions and heroic dreams.	**7**
7	Sport provides places for fans to become positively active members of intimately engaged communities.	**7**
8	Sport enables its participants to build work-ready capabilities that result in high-wage jobs.	**7**
9	Sport engagement lowers the incidence of juvenile crime by giving young people something to aspire to.	**6**
10	Sport builds character by turning callow youths into responsible and civic-minded adults.	**6**
11	Sport is an ideal site for promoting social causes and changing social behaviour.	**5**
12	Sport is a safety valve for the release of pent-up aggression and hostility.	**3**
13	The sporting achievements of elite athletes create positive role models for emulation by young people.	**2**
14	Sport provides safe and protective spaces for securing exhilarating experiences.	**2**
15	Sport makes its participants morally virtuous by having them deal with conflicted choices.	**1**

Table 5.3 PVP Situational Matrix

	Achievability	
	LOW	*HIGH*
LOW	Scores of 0–4	Scores of 6–7
Stakeholder Support		
HIGH	Scores of 3–5	Scores of 8–10

So, what do these scorecards, ratings, and diagrammatic comparisons tell us about sport's ability to create public value? At first glance it appears that its value-building capacity has been over-rated. But is this really the case, and have we missed something that paints a quite different picture?

Notes

1 A fascinating study into sport's societal impacts and their conversion into public value propositions (PVPs) is contained in Willem der Roest and Bake Dijk (2021). Developing an elite sports' public value proposition in Northern Netherlands, *European Sport Management Quarterly,* 21 (5): 677–694.

2 Bob Stewart and Aaron C.T. Smith (2025). *Levelling the Playing Field: The Problem with Sport and What Can Be Done About It,* Australian Scholarly Publishing.

3 John Phillips and Walter Schafer (1971). Consequences of participation in interscholastic sports: A review and prospectus, *The Pacific Sociological Review*, 14: 328–338.

4 Erah Ali, Kaitlyn Constantino, Azah Hussain, and Zaibar Akhtar (2018). The effects of play-based learning on early childhood education and development, *Journal of Evolution of Medical and Dental Sciences*, 7 (43): Online publication. See also Ngan Kuen Lai, Tan Fong Ang, Lip Yee Por, and Chee Sun Liew (2018). The impact of play on child development - A literature review, *European Early Childhood Education Research Journal*, 26 (4): 1–19.

5 Diann Eley and David Kirk (2002). Developing citizenship through sport: The impact of a sport-based volunteer programme on young sport leader, *Sport, Education and Society,* 7 (2): 151–166.

6 Carreres Ponsoda, Federico Amparo, Escartí Carbonell, Juan Cortell-Tormo, Vicent Fuster-Lloret and Eliseo Andreu (2012). The relationship between out-of-school sport participation and positive youth development, *Journal of Human Sport and Exercise*, 7 (3): 671–683.

7 Alfonso Valero Valenzuela, Ernesto De la Cruz Sánchez, Alberto Gómez-Mármol, and Bernardino Javier Sánchez-Alcaraz Martinez (2017). Personal and social responsibility development through sport participation in youth scholars, *Journal of Physical Education and Sport,* 17 (2): 775–782.

8 Nicholas Holt, Kacey Neely, Linda Slater, Martin Camiré, Jean Côté, Jessica Fraser-Thomas, Dany MacDonald, Leisha Strachan, and Katherine Tamminen (2017). A grounded theory of positive youth development through sport based on results from a qualitative meta-study, *International Review of Sport and Exercise Psychology,* 10 (1): 1–49.

9 Christiana Bessa, Peter Hastie, Rui Araújo, and Isabel Mesquita (2019). What do we know about the development of personal and social skills within the sport

education model: A systematic review, *Journal of Sports Science & Medicine*, 18 (4): 812–829.

10 As many researchers and commentators have noted, character development is a 'lifelong, holistic process… primarily influenced by contextual variables throughout a person's life.' Sport is but one of many factors that might influence a young person's character development. For a detailed exposition around this theme, see Joseph Doty (2000). Sports build character?! *Journal of College & Character*, 7 (3). Online publication.

11 Maria Kavussanu and Christopher Ring (2016). Moral thought and action in sport and student life: A study of bracketed morality, *Ethics & Behavior*, 26: 267–276.

12 Brenda Jo Bredemeier and David Shields (1984). Divergence in Moral reasoning about sport and everyday life. *Sociology of Sport Journal,* 1 (4): 348–357.

13 Thomas Perks (2007). Does sport foster social capital? The contribution of sport to a lifestyle of community participation, *Sociology of Sport Journal*, 24 (4): 378–401.

14 If you want to go deep into the theory of social capital and its application to different sport settings, we recommend you read Matthew Nicholson and Russell Hoye (2008). *Sport and Social Capital,* Routledge; and Richard Tacon (2022). *Social Capital and Sport Organisations*, Routledge.

15 Gareth Wiltshire and Clare Stevinson (2017). Exploring the role of social capital in community-based physical activity: Qualitative insights from a parkrun, *Qualitative Research in Sport*, 10 (7): 1–16.

16 Margaret Lawler, Caroline Heary, and Elizabeth Nixon (2020). Peer support and role modelling predict physical activity change among adolescents over twelve months, *Journal of Youth and Adolescence,* 49: 1503–1516.

17 John Lyle (2009). *Sporting Success, Role Models and Participation: A Policy Related Review Research Report no. 101*, Sport Scotland.

18 John Amaechi (2020). *Sports Stars are Held up as Role Models – Until They Want to Stand up to Racism*. The Guardian, 29 August.

19 Veerle de Bosscher, Popi Sotiriadou, and Maarten van Bottenburg (2013). Scrutinizing the sport pyramid metaphor: An examination of the relationship between elite success and mass participation in Flanders, *International Journal of Sport Policy and Politics,* 5 (3): 319–339.

20 Douglas Hartmann and Brooks Depro (2006). Rethinking sports-based community crime prevention: A preliminary analysis of the relationship between midnight basketball and urban crime rates, *Journal of Sport and Social Issues*, 30 (2): 180–196.

21 Margot Gardner, Jodie Roth, and Jeanne Brooks-Gunn. (2009). Sports participation and juvenile delinquency: The role of the peer context among adolescent boys and girls with varied histories of problem behavior, *Developmental Psychology*, 45 (2): 341.

22 See, for example, Ricardo Sabates (2008). Educational attainment and juvenile crime: Area-level evidence using three cohorts of young people, *The British Journal of Criminology,* 48 (3): 395–409; Iryna Rud, Chris van Klaveren, Wim Groot, and H. Maassenvandenbrink (2013). Education and youth crime: A review of the empirical literature, Tier Working Paper Series, January. Online publication; Roderik Rekker, Dustin Pardini, Loes Keijsers, Susan Branje, Rolf Loeber, and Wim Meeus (2015). Moving in and out of poverty: The within-individual association between socioeconomic status and juvenile delinquency, *PLOS ONE* 10 (11). Online publication; and John Pitts (2020). Black young people and gang involvement in London, *Youth Justice*, 20 (1–2): 146–158.

23 See, for instance, Irina Jugl, Doris Bender, and Friedrich Lösel (2021). Do sports programs prevent crime and reduce reoffending? A systematic review and meta-analysis on the effectiveness of sports programs, *Journal of Quantitative Criminology*, 6 November. Online publication.

24 For a succinct overview, which confirms that being physically active increases the probability of being happy, see Zhanjia Zhang and Weiyun Chen (2019). Systematic review of the relationship between physical activity and happiness, *Journal of Happiness Studies*, 20 (4): 1305–1322. This positive relationship cut across not only observational studies (cross-sectional and longitudinal) but also intervention studies (including both randomised controlled trials and non-randomised trials). But the researchers also reminded us that we 'cannot draw firm conclusions regarding the causal relationship between physical activity and happiness.'

25 Frey, Bruno S. and Gullo, Anthony (2021). Does sports make people happier, or do happy people do more sports? *Journal of Sports Economics*, 22 (4): 432–458.

26 Jeeyoon Kim and David Jeffrey (2019). Sport and happiness: Understanding the relations among sport consumption activities, long-and short-term subjective well-being, and psychological need fulfilment, *Journal of Sport Management*, 33 (2): 119–132.

27 Hyun-Woo Lee, Sun Yun Shin, Kyle Bunds, Minjung Kim, and Kwang Min Cho (2014). Rediscovering the positive psychology of sport participation: Happiness in a ski resort context, *Applied Research in Quality of Life*, 9: 575–590.

28 Tim Pawlowski, Paul Downward, and Simona Rasciute (2011). Subjective well-being in European countries - On the age-specific impact of physical activity, *European Review of Aging and Physical Activity*, 8 (2): 93–102.

29 Jennifer Pharr and Nancy Lough (2016). Examining the relationship between sport and health among USA women: An analysis of the behavioral risk factor surveillance system, *Journal of Sport and Health Science*, 5 (4): 403–409.

30 Lindsay Taliaferro, Barbara Rienzo, and Kristine Donovan (2010). Relationships between youth sport participation and selected health risk behaviors from 1999 to 2007, *Journal of School Health*, 80 (8): 399–410.

31 Korcz Agata and Makama Monyeki (2018). Association between sport participation, body composition, physical fitness, and social correlates among adolescents: The PAHL study, *International Journal of Environmental Research and Public Health*, 15 (12): 2793–2809.

32 Pekka Oja, Paul Kelly, Zeljko Pedisic, Sylvia Titze, Adrian Bauman, Charlie Foster, Mark Hamer, Melvyn Hillsdon, and Emmanuel Stamatakis (2016). Associations of specific types of sports and exercise with all-cause and cardiovascular-disease mortality: A cohort study of 80306 British adults, *British Journal of Sports Medicine*, 51 (10). Online publication.

33 Molly Easterlin, Paul Chung, Mei Leng, and Rebecca Dudovitz, (2019). Association of team sports participation with long-term mental health outcomes among individuals exposed to adverse childhood experiences, *JAMA Paediatrics*, 173 (7): 681–688.

34 A research study found that increased physical activity levels had assisted in the management of post-traumatic stress disorders and bouts of agoraphobia. For details, see Filipe Such, Brendon Stubbs, Jacob Meyer, Andreas Heissel, Philipp Zech, Davy Vancampfort, Simon Rosenbaum, Jeroen Deenik, Joseph Firth, Philip B. Ward, Andre F. Carvalho, and Sarah A. Hiles (2019). Physical activity protects from incident anxiety: A meta-analysis of prospective cohort studies, *Depression and Anxiety*. Online publication.

35 Unfortunately, there are, as we speak, signs that things are getting worse. A 2021 study of Danish female and male youth soccer players revealed many psychological disorders. Around 20% of them disclosed moderate or severe symptoms of common mental disorders, with anxiety front and centre. In addition, female soccer players were more likely to experience symptoms of mental illness than male youth players while also being likely to experience lower 'mental well-being.' The study is available in Andreas Kuettel, Natalie Durand-Bush, and Carsten Larsen (2021).

Mental health profiles of Danish youth soccer players: The influence of gender and career development, *Journal of Clinical Sport Psychology*, 16 (3): 276–293. But worse was yet to come. A 2022 study of 115 elite female English soccer players found that 36% displayed eating disorder symptoms, 11% displayed moderate-to-severe anxiety symptoms, and 11% displayed moderate-to-severe depression symptoms. For all the details and more, see Carly Perry, Aiden Chauntry, and Francesca Champ (2022). Elite female footballers in England: An exploration of mental ill-health and help-seeking intentions, *Science and Medicine in Football,* 6 (5): 650–659.

36 See, for example, Katja Siefken, Astrid Junge, and Lena Lämmle (2019). How does sport affect mental health? An investigation into the relationship of leisure-time physical activity with depression and anxiety, *Human Movement*, 20 (1): 62–74. Siefken and her colleagues found that participants who had met the World Health Organisation recommendations for healthy living (moderate-intensity physical activity for 150 minutes a week) had reduced symptoms of depression and anxiety. Similar conclusions were drawn 15 years earlier by Monika Guszkowska (2004). Effects of exercise on anxiety, depression and mood, *Psychiatria Polska*, 38 (4): 611–620. Guszkowska found that the most dramatic improvements were the result of rhythmic and aerobic exercises, the use of large muscle groups when jogging, swimming, cycling, walking, and doing it all at moderate and low intensity for 15–30 minutes three times a week for at least 10 weeks. She went on to say that changes in anxiety, depression, and mood states after exercise were best explained by the monoamine hypotheses, which involves the actions of a group of neurotransmitters including dopamine, serotonin, and endorphins. They can impact positively on the psychological state of people, especially during and immediately after exercise. Dopamine is released in the anticipation of a pleasurable experience, which in turn heightens the experience. Serotonin regulates mood. Endorphins are natural painkillers that not only reduce discomfort but also elevate well-being. Outdoor and adventure education programmes can also deliver psychological and mental health benefits. One study found that participants 'scored higher in life satisfaction, happiness, mindfulness, and self-efficacy and lower in perceived stress' after having spent eight days in the Norwegian wilderness. For details, see Michael Mutz and Johannes Müller (2016). Mental health benefits of outdoor adventures: Results from two pilot studies, *Journal of Adolescence*, 49: 105–114.

37 Vincent Gouttebarge, Frank Backx, Haruhito Aoki, and Gino Kerkhoffs (2015). Symptoms of common mental disorders in professional football (soccer) across five European countries, *Journal of Sports Science and Medicine*, 14 (4): 811–818.

38 Hannah Newman, Karen Howells, and David Fletcher (2016). The dark side of top-level sport: An autobiographic study of depressive experiences in elite sport performers, *Frontiers in Psychology*, 7 (868): Online publication.

39 Simon Rice, Rosemary Purcell, Stefanie De Silva, Daveena Mawren, Patrick D. McGorry, and Alexandra G. Parker (2016). The mental health of elite athletes: A narrative systematic review. *Sports Medicine*, 46 (9): 1333–1353.

40 It appears that the only situation in which participant aggression – especially where adolescents are involved – dissipates in any regular way is where an 'intervention programme has been specifically designed to alleviate this tendency, But even here, the results vary. Whereas team sport activities often lowered aggression levels, gym-based activities rarely did. For all the details, see Yuxin Zhu, Jianbin Li, Mengge Zhang, Chunxiao Li, Eva Yi Hung Lau, and Sisi Tao (2022). Physical activity participation and physical aggression in children and adolescents: A systematic review and meta-analysis, *Psychology of Sport and Exercise*, 63 (November). Online publication..

41 Tarkinton Newman, Erica Magier and Carlyn Kimiecik (2021). The relationship between youth sport participation and the onset of and/or adherence to aggressive and violent behavior: A scoping review of the literature, *Journal of the Society of Social Work and Research*, May. Online. publication

42 James Curtis, William McTeer, and Philip White (2003). Do high school athletes earn more pay? Youth sport participation and earnings as an adult, *Sociology of Sport Journal*, 20 (1): 60–76.

43 Michael Lechner (2009). Long-run labour market and health effects of individual sports activities, *Journal of Health Economics*, 28 (4): 839–854.

44 A good attempt to explain this phenomenon was made by Michael Lechner in a 2015 paper written for the *IZA World of Labour* agency. Lechner developed a process model of worker productivity that had (1) soft emotional-capital social skills, (2) hard human-capital technical skills), (3) physical appearance, and (4) health levels as the key drivers of worker productivity. Lechner argued that at least three of these four drivers could be enhanced by playing sport, doing exercise, and engaging in some form of regular physical recreation. So, Lechner was able to argue that fit, healthy, socially adept, skilled, and physically attractive workers were more productive than those who were not, and thus more deserving of a pay rise. QED to Lechner. For a full explanation of what Lechner had to say go to Michael Lechner (2015). Sports, exercise, and labor market outcomes. increasing participation in sports and exercise can boost productivity, IZA *World of Labor*, February. Sports, exercise, and labor market outcomes (iza.org)

45 Further reinforcement for this conclusion was found in Kelvin Mwita and Eliza Mwakasangula (2019). The role of sports participation on graduate employability, *Journal of Management Research and Analysis*, 6 (4): 159–163.

46 In early 2023, a KPMG report into female executives in Ireland found that nine out of ten Irish businesswomen believed the skills they had learned through sport were not only transferable to the workplace but had also made them better managers. The most cited transferable skills were teamwork (90%), confidence (86%), and self-belief (63%). For more details, go to Sport and women's careers - KPMG Ireland (home.kpmg).

47 John Bradbury, Dennis Coates, and Brad Humphreys (2022). The Impact of professional sports franchises and venues on local economies: A comprehensive survey, *Journal of Economic Surveys*, 31 January. Online publication; Kaveephong Lertwachara and James Cochran (2007). An event study of the economic impact of professional sport franchises on local us economies, *Journal of Sports Economics*, 8 (3): 244–254.

48 For a comprehensive overview of the mechanics of cost-benefit analysis and the processes involved, especially when assessing cultural and sporting events, see Sanja Tišma, Mira Mileusnić, Škrtić, Sanja Maleković, and Daniela Angelina Jelinčić (2021). Cost–benefit analysis in the evaluation of cultural heritage project funding, *Journal of Risk and Financial Management,* 14: 466. Online publication.

49 For a comprehensive overview of the mechanics of cost-benefit analysis and the processes involved, especially when assessing cultural and sporting events, see Sanja Tišma, Mira Mileusnić, Škrtić, Sanja Maleković, and Daniela Angelina Jelinčić (2021). Cost–benefit analysis in the evaluation of cultural heritage project funding, *Journal of Risk and Financial Management,* 14: 466. Online publication.

50 For a highly critical analysis of the ways in which the benefits of big sport events can be magnified – and the costs either marginalised or just excluded – to get a positive outcome, see John Rennie Short (2020). *Hosting the Olympic Games: The Real Cost for Cities*, Routledge. Short identified several factors that were often ignored by the host city/town organisers when measuring the net benefit. They included the

level of government borrowings, accumulated debt, environmental damage, disruption and loss of amenity, congestion, and even corruption.

51 Larissa Davies (2002). Sport in the city: Measuring economic significance at the local level, *European Sport Management Quarterly,* 2 (2): 83–112.

52 Camila de Vengoechea (2012). Sports as a tool for social change. *World Economic Forum,* 19 April. Sports as a tool for social change | World Economic Forum (weforum.org)

53 Jack Mahony (2022). Qatar World Cup organiser Hassan Al-Thawadi admits more than 400 migrant workers died building infrastructure. *Skynews. com.au,* 30 November. https://www.skynews.com.au/australia-news/sport/qatar-world-cup-organiser-hassan-althawadi-admits-more-than-400-migrant-workers-died-building-infrastructure/news-story/097b1d1b02330a891499e0084dcef3a7

54 Jamie Cleland, Stacey Pope, and John Williams (2020). 'I do worry that football will become over-feminized': Ambiguities in fan reflections on the gender order in men's professional football in the United Kingdom, *Sociology of Sport Journal*, 37 (4): 366–375.

55 Brigid McCarthy (2022). 'Who unlocked the kitchen?': Online misogyny, YouTube comments and women's professional street skateboarding, *International Review for the Sociology of Sport*, 57 (3): 362–380.

56 Sarah Barnes and Mary Louise Adams (2022). A large and troubling iceberg: sexism and misogyny in women's work as sport coaches, *Sports Coaching Review*, 11 (2): 127–146.

57 Karin Boczek, Leyla Dogruel, and Christiana Schallhorn (2022). Gender byline bias in sports reporting: Examining the visibility and audience perception of male and female journalists in sports coverage, *Journalism*, 2 January. Online publication.

58 Daniel Kilvington, Kevin Hylton, Jonathan Long, and Alex Bond (2022). Investigating online football forums: A critical examination of participants' responses to football related racism and Islamophobia, *Soccer & Society.* Online publication.

59 John Obinna Onwe (2016). Involuntary emotions: Exploring the experiences of winning and losing on sport fans, *International Journal of Sport Studies*, 6: 136–146.

60 Elizabeth Delia, Jeffrey James, and Daniel Wann. (2021). Does being a sport fan provide meaning in life? *Journal of Sport Management,* 36 (1): 45–55.

61 For an insightful case study see Alain Brechbühl, Annemarie Schumacher Dimech, and Roland Seiler (2020). Policing football fans in Switzerland - A case study involving fans, stadium security employees, and police officers, *Policing: A Journal of Policy and Practice*, 14 (4): 865–882.

62 Lukasz Kuźma, Krzysztof Struniawski, Piotr Sielatycki, Szymon Pogorzelski Szymon, Hanna Bachórzewska-Gajewska, and Hanna Dobrzycki (2020). It is not just a game. Do soccer matches affect cardiovascular events? *Archives of Medical Science*, 16 (1): 1–8.

63 Charles Hillman, Bruce Cuthbert, James Cauraugh, Harald Schupp, Margaret Bradley, and Peter Lang (2000). Psychophysiological responses of sport fans, *Motivation and Emotion*, 24 (1): 13–28.

64 Walter Gantz, Zheng Wang, Paul Bryant, and Robert Potter (2006). Sports versus all comers: Comparing TV sports fans with fans of other programming genres, *Journal of Broadcasting & Electronic Media*, 50 (1): 95–118.

65 If you want more evidence, then go to David Kesler and Daniel Wann (2020). The well-being of sport fans: Predicting personal life satisfaction and social life satisfaction, *Journal of Sport Behaviour*, 43 (3): Online publication. A 2021 study (Yuran Su, James Du, Rui Biscaia, and Yuhei Inoue. We are in this together: Sport brand involvement and fans' well-being, *European Sport Management Quarterly.* October (Online publication) had a similar story to tell. The authors found that fans'

involvement with sport brands – that is, teams – was positively associated with fans' psychological well-being by giving them a sense of togetherness, and thus 'mitigating any potential sense of loss.' Clearly some fans were easily pleased.

66 For a comprehensive theory of sport's cognitive features based on brain science see Aaron C.T. Smith (2023). *Football on the Brain: Why Minds Love Sport.* Margin Press.

67 Michael Novak (1976). *The Joy of Sport: Endzones, Bases, Baskets, Balls, and the Consecration of the American Spirit*, Madison Books.

68 Toben Nelson and Harold Wechsler (2001). Alcohol and college athletes, *Medicine and Science in Sports and Exercise*, 33 (1): 43–47.

69 Olivier de Hon, Harm Kuipers, and Maarten van Bottenburg, (2015). Prevalence of doping use in elite sports: A review of numbers and methods, *Sports Medicine*, 45 (1): 57–69; Rolf Ulrich, Harrison PopeJr, Léa Cléret, Andrea Petróczi, Tamás Nepusz, Jay Schaffer, Gen Kanayama, Dawn Comstock, and Perikles Simon (2018). Doping in two elite athletics competitions assessed by randomized-response surveys, *Sports Medicine*, 48 (1): 211–219.

70 The violence-in-sport problem, especially in professional competitions, was well understood as far back as 40–50 years ago. Richard Burrows, a prominent American sports lawyer, discovered that for the final few years of the 1970s, more than 17 million sport-related injuries were reported annually, with many being the result of violent 'on field' acts. In Richard's mind, it was as if 'the mere act of putting on a uniform and entering the sports arena [served] as a license to engage in behaviour which would constitute a crime if committed elsewhere.' Cited in Richard Borrows (1982). Violence in professional sports: Is it part of the game? *Journal of Legislation*, 9 (1): Article 1.

71 See for instance Lynn Jamieson and Thomas Orr (2009). *Sport and Violence: A Critical Examination of Sport*, Routledge; and Kevin Young (2019). *Sport, Violence and Society Second Edition*, Routledge.

72 For an illuminating overview of ice hockey in North America, and the nexus between injuries and violence, see Greg Anderson, Heath Melugin, and Michael Stuart (2019). Epidemiology of injuries in ice hockey. *Sport Health*, 11 (6): 514–519; Shaun Rudd, James Hodge, Rachael Finley, Peter Lewis, and Michael Wang (2016). Should we ban boxing? *BMJ*, 352: 389. Online publication.

73 For further details see Reynald Lastra, Peter Bell, and Christine Bond (2016). Sports betting-motivated corruption in Australia: An under-studied phenomenon, *International Journal of Social Science Research*, 4 (1): 62–82; The problem seemed to be particularly virulent when it came to 'live' or 'in play' betting. For more details see Elizabeth Killick and Mark Griffiths (2020). Why do individuals engage in in-play sports betting? A qualitative interview study, *Journal of Gambling Issues*, 37: 221–240.

74 Australian Parliament (2022). *Parliamentary Inquiry into Repeated Head Trauma in Contact Sports.* December. Concussions and repeated head trauma in contact sports – Parliament of Australia (aph.gov.au).

75 UK Parliament (2021). *Committee of Inquiry into Concussion in Sport.* February. Concussion in sport - Committees - UK Parliament.

76 Hagar Cohen, Alex McDonald, Alice Mulheron, and Dan Harrison (2023). Paralympic athletes and officials call for action on cheating and intentional misrepresentation. *ABC News/Four Corners*, 4 April. Earlier paralympic scandals were revealed in Darren Mara and Emily Jane Smith (2021). Cheating in the paralympics: The fight for fairness? *SBS News/Dateline*, 21 August. Simon Maybin and Esperanza Escribano (2021). Fake paralympians boss: 'I didn't know about cheating'. *BBC World Service*, 19 September.

77 Swathes of detail can be found in Sarah Jewell and James Reade (2020). On fixing international cricket matches, *The Journal of Gambling Business and Economics,* 13 (2): 37–82; and Zia Akhtar (2017). Match fixing, illegal gambling, and cricket in the Indian subcontinent, *The Entertainment and Sports Lawyer*, 33 (4): Online publication.

78 See, for example, Fuhua Huang, Wenyan Xiao, and Huijie Zhang (2018). Not all 'the evils of capitalism': Match-fixing and the governance of Chinese professional football, 1994–2016, *The International Journal of the History of Sport*, 35 (2–3): 277–292; Serhat Yilmaz, Argyro Elisavet Manoli, and Georgios Antonopoulos (2018). An anatomy of Turkish football match-fixing, *Trends in Organised Crime*, May 1–19. Online publication.

79 Jens De Rycke and Veerle De Bosscher (2021). The cure or the cause? Public opinions of elite sports' societal benefits and harms, *Sport in Society*, 24 (7): 1070–1092.

80 The results for each of the 79 items are listed in pp. 1078–1080

6 The Capital Value of Sport

Capital and Costs

Having reflected long and hard on the scorecard ratings we provided in Chapter 5, we found them troublesome for two reasons. First, many of the 15 proposed benefits ascribed to sport – which we retitled as PVPs – were not always achieved. In other instances, they were conditional, realised only when accompanied by interventions that involved good planning, sound administration, and skilled instruction. In short, it appeared that sport's 'natural' ability to make society a better place had been exaggerated. Second, commentators and analysts often failed to consider the costs that occurred along the way. As we went deep into our interrogation of the claims made about sport's ability to make us all better off, we discovered plenty of downsides.

To sharpen our understanding of the scores we gave to each of the 15 PVPs we constructed, we will now view them through the conceptual lens of capital accumulation. The question that follows is: has sport added to the capital stocks of society, and consequently improved citizen well-being, or has it insidiously stripped away some of the most precious forms of capital and thus diminished citizen well-being? Let's see what our analysis reveals.

Capital Accumulation

The use of the term capital as a way of understanding how individuals and society go about building their wealth, well-being, and quality of life has a strong intellectual pedigree. The foundation work began with the English political economist, Adam Smith, who in the 18th century examined the concepts of physical and economic capital. Things progressed with the American economist, Theodore Schultz, in the 1960s, who promoted the idea of human capital.

This human capital approach was subsequently adapted by the international development researcher, Amartya Sen, who introduced the concept of human capabilities, and broadened by the analysis of the French sociologist, Pierre Bourdieu, during the 1970s and 1980s. Bourdieu argued that capital –

DOI: 10.4324/9781003546931-6

and the power it delivered to its beneficiaries – went far beyond economic and human capital by including cultural, symbolic, and social aspects.[1] His ground-breaking research into how capital was accumulated and how it added value was detailed in his 1979 book *Distinction,* which demonstrated how cultural capital was distributed in French society and why some citizens had a lot, while others had very little.[2]

The ways in which social capital adds value to society were popularised by Robert Putnam in 2000 with the publication of *Bowling Alone*.[3] Putnam found that American society had become increasingly disconnected from family, friends, neighbours, and its democratic structures. As a result, its stock of social capital had plummeted and, in doing so, impoverished communities. Over the last 20 years or so, we have witnessed an explosive expansion of the different types of societal capital, with human/intellectual,[4] psychological,[5] emotional,[6] natural,[7] and spiritual[8] having secured significant conceptual space.

The widespread use of capital accumulation models to assess societal well-being provides us with both the confidence and opportunity to do two things. The first is to reveal the ways in which sport has helped build society's capital stocks and thus increase society's wealth and overall well-being. The second is to see if sport may also have done the opposite, which is to strip society of some of its capital stocks and wealth, and thus diminish well-being.

We must concede, though, that this approach can be problematic. The first problem is that when assessing conceptual measures like capital, value, and wealth, it is easy to jettison benefits that cannot be monetised (that is, given a specific monetary value). However, we have made strenuous efforts to include even the most intangible and ephemeral factors.

The second problem is that not all benefits will have the same social significance or 'weight.' For instance, there is no simple formula that can tell us the differential impact of an improvement in a youth's mental toughness on one hand and the 'feel good' mood associated with a community sport event on the other. This weakness cannot be easily resolved so long as some factors cannot be readily converted to monetary values or material measures.

The third problem relates to the cost/liability side of the capital ledger. Many costs are even more obtuse than the benefits. Further complications arise when having to decide how much weight to give matters like on-field violence, gender discrimination, gambling addiction, and the stresses associated with hyper-competition. Monetising them is possible but contestable at all steps. But despite these limitations, we went with this approach in the absence of a better alternative.

Interpersonal Capital

Let's begin with the notion of interpersonal capital – or social capital as it is often called – which has to do with the friendships people make and the network of relationships they have built. Interpersonal/social capital has been positioned as a crucial indicator of individual and community well-being, especially when it breaks down barriers and integrates minority groups into the broader society.[9] The evidence we reviewed on social connections and on fandom suggests that sport has a unique ability to bring people together. It also works at different levels, be it the neighbourhood, the local community, or even the nation. Furthermore, it goes well beyond being a member of a sporting club in claiming the attention of fans whose collective passions have few limits. It enables people to seamlessly assimilate into social groups by providing safe spaces for light conversation, harmless banter, and even serious debate. It can also break down social barriers and bring diverse communities closer together.[10] It would be reasonable to conclude that if you want to make friends and expand your social network, then you should join a sports club. But we found that not everyone secured positive outcomes. Being good at the game and having a 'bubbly' and/or outgoing personality enabled some participants to secure more friends than those with timid dispositions.

Economic Capital

We need to consider the contribution sport makes to the stock of economic capital. Economic capital connects to workplace earnings and localised economic impacts. Somewhat surprisingly, sport participation was – with very few exceptions – associated with higher income levels, although it was more significant for men than women. When it came to assessing sport's impact on local economies through additional spending, more jobs, and improved infrastructure, the results were generally positive. However, in many cases, the net addition to economic capital was far less impressive. This was because large parts of the stimulus were the result of government spending, which meant that other community services like libraries, parklands, and public transport were not as well funded as they could have been. On balance, though, the stocks of economic capital at both the individual and community levels were enhanced by sport's presence.[11]

Educational/Cultural Capital

We have labelled our next form of capital educational/cultural. Educational/cultural capital includes all those learning experiences that enhance one's cognitive capability or expand one's knowledge base while adding to the collective intelligence of communities and nations.[12] Communities with high levels of educational and cultural capital will be regarded as technologically advanced, worldly, well-read, artistically inclined, interested in ideas, and fashionably tasteful. The research examining the relationship between sport participation and educational attainment was strangely ambivalent or ambiguous. While some of the studies found that students who played sport achieved better academic results than those who did not, it was not clear that sport was the cause of the difference. Greater self-discipline and a more positive attitude to school in general may have been contributing factors. Further, when it came to girls, sport engagement was mostly of little significance. To sum up, sport participation sometimes led to better school grades but rarely led to lower grades. In short, playing sport did not lower academic achievement, but neither was it a guaranteed pathway to higher grades. When it came to cultural capital, we were left clutching at straws. Having noted the findings that people who played sport earned, on average, higher incomes than those who did not, we tentatively concluded that a significant part of these earnings would be spent on culturally and intellectually uplifting experiences.

Psychological Capital

We had to give space to the concept of psychological capital. Psychological capital can take on many forms. However, in the context of this book and the issues it addresses, we decided to highlight the ways in which sport engagement can make individuals and communities more emotionally stable, mentally tough, socially adaptable, and happier with their lives. We considered the claim that sport builds character, and we examined the ways in which sport makes people happy, including the proposition that sport provides a buffer against severe psychological disorders. The results were mixed. When it came to character building, the evidence showed that it was a hit-and-miss affair with sport delivering on its promises only when it had the participant's social development as a priority. When it came to happiness, there were marginal gains from playing sport. As far as psychological disorders were concerned, children and adolescents who were exposed to well-administered sports programmes had a greater chance of becoming relatively well-adjusted adults who could manage stress and exhibit emotional resilience. At the same time, there were no studies which found that sport participation was a universal panacea for unhappiness, low self-esteem, emotional fragility, chronic stress, anxiety, or depression. Moreover, in hyper-competitive settings, the threat of public humiliation and severe psychological harm was ever present.[13] On balance, though, sport engagement added more to a society's stocks of psychological capital than it stripped away.[14]

Moral Capital

Whenever sport is mentioned in general conversation, the notions of 'fair play and sports(wo)manship' inevitably arise. The argument goes that sport provides lifelong lessons about the difference between what is right and wrong and what is fair and unfair. In short, doing sport is supposed to make its participants 'morally virtuous' and will thus expand a community's stocks of moral capital.[15] Like social capital, the evidence was in, but unlike social capital, the findings were not flattering. There were a multitude of cases where violence, cheating, and insidious gameplay had destroyed the integrity of sport and squeezed all the fun and exhilaration out of it for nearly everybody.[16] While the character-building studies explained the theory behind sport's influence on shaping the temperament and behaviour of young people, the evidence in support of it was slight. In fact, there was little to no evidence to support the claim that role models had any lasting positive influence on impressionable children and adolescents. We were forced to conclude that sport's capacity for inculcating its participants with a strong ethical grounding and clearly defined moral guidelines was close to zero. On the other hand, its potential to inflict moral harm was significant, especially when participants were perfectionists, narcissists, opportunists, and driven by an obsessive desire to win.[17]

Physical Capital

Physical capital is fundamentally about body, health, fitness, and longevity.[18] The studies concerning sport and longevity reinforced the now axiomatic claim that sport participation had a positive effect on health and life span. It not only guards against non-transmittable diseases and enables people to be more active but also slows down the ageing process. A sedentary lifestyle sounds both courageously romantic and dangerously decadent, but it is also a recipe for early entry into a nursing home and a premature death.[19] It additionally exerts considerable pressures on a nation's health care system.[20] However, the evidence we reviewed also highlighted some negative behaviours associated with regular sports engagement. Team sport participants were more likely to use smokeless tobacco and binge drink than non-participants. Sport participants also had a higher risk of disordered eating. But we were not prepared to say that sport's capacity to build healthy communities was overrated. Rather, these 'deviant' behaviours were, in the scheme of things, little more than irritants that were already being dealt with through a swag of health promotion programmes.

Civic Capital

We decided that the concept of civic capital deserved a space of its own.[21] In several studies, reference was made to sports' capacity to change the ways in which young people engaged with their communities, including the relationships between sport and character building, sport and delinquency, sport and psychological resilience, and sport and fandom. As far as character building and its relationship with civic engagement were concerned, a couple of studies found that where sport-related programmes were infused with the idea that sport can build responsible citizens, civic engagement mostly followed. Similar findings were found in the section on psychological resilience. Some of the fandom studies also showed how civic pride and well-being were enhanced when a community event was well attended, a local team did well, or a local hero excelled on the national or international stage.[22] When it came to sport's ability to change the beliefs and attitudes of wayward youth, numerous studies indicated that some at-risk adolescents were able to change their life direction. Instead of identifying with gangs and violently rebelling against society's norms, their experience with sport gave them a window into new ways of connecting with the wider world. However, in some instances the risky appeal of hyper-masculine lifestyles overwhelmed any opportunity to positively contribute to the life of their local communities by doing good and making a difference. Also in some cases, the intensely competitive nature of sport encouraged young participants to be more aggressive, petulant, and ruthless. Taking all things into account, sport added slightly more to civic capital than it took away.

Protective Capital

Having accounted for civic capital, we determined that a gap around the theme of protective capital remained.[23] While it mainly related to a sense of feeling safe, it extended into the harms that resulted from engaging in sport.[24] This issue was signalled from earlier analyses, where it was proposed that while sport gave people enormous joy, it also came with risks and costs, with some sports being more risky and costlier than others. These risks and costs encompass the connections between sport and happiness, sport and psychological resilience, sport and stress relief, sport and social progress, sport and fandom, and sport and risk reduction.

When it came to sport's relationship with resilience, stress, and anxiety, the impact of sport proved disturbing. At the elite level, chronic stress was associated with various forms of mental disorders, with many professional athletes seeking refuge by removing themselves from the public gaze altogether. In addition, sport was not a social safety valve for the harmless dissipation of pent-up anger, since on-field aggression frequently leaked into off-field settings. Fan behaviour was also subject to negative spillover effects, where the excitement of the game (or eustress, as it is sometimes called) could quickly turn into violence, especially when alcohol was involved. Excessive eustress was also a problem for older men by increasing the risk of heart failure.

These proved to be just the tip of the sport-risk iceberg. Performance-enhancing drug use was rampant; licit drugs – with alcohol and painkillers dominant – were endemic; the threat of violence was always lurking beneath the game-day surface; contact and adventure sports had massive injury rates; and gambling became addictive amongst many sport followers. It did not end there since we also found that racism was embedded in the sporting landscape, homophobia was bubbling just beneath the surface, while misogyny and sexism were still evident in conversational sub-texts. Sexual abuse, including paedophilia, was also found in sports where older men – especially those with coaching responsibilities and mentoring roles – had close relationships with younger athletes. Swimming[25] and gymnastics[26] were especially problematic.[27]

All these problems paled into insignificance with the publication of a pioneering Australian study. It found that when the local health benefits of sport participation were balanced against the injury costs incurred in securing them, the costs outweighed the benefits. And, having discovered recent research that showed increased participation in heavy-contact sports was associated with increased levels of violent and property crimes in early adolescence,[28] we were forced to conclude that instead of building up society's protective capital, sport was stripping it away. On the evidence, sport presented a threat to the safety of a society's citizens.

Social Justice Capital

We have called the final element social justice capital.[29] Our reflections on the studies related to this area confirmed that in recent times, sport had taken on a new and important, but quite onerous, role.[30] By the 2020s, sport had become an important vehicle for communicating socio-political – often called 'social cause' or 'social justice' – messages.[31] Sport marketing professionals had also gotten into the act by linking social causes and social justice issues to social marketing and cause-related marketing, and locating them under the corporate social responsibility banner.[32] While these types of initiatives were not new – the 1968 black power/black glove salute by USA athletes Tommie Smith and John Carlos at a track and field medal ceremony at the Mexico Olympic Games was an iconic incident[33] – its scale has increased exponentially over the last 20 years or so.[34]

One exemplar, the Australian Football League, began pursuing a 'social cause' agenda during the 2010s, which included a 'national inclusion' football carnival for people with an intellectual disability, coaching forums targeted at women, a 'Flying Boomerang' development and leadership course for young Indigenous players, a football development programmes for young Muslim males, a 'gender action plan' to improve gender equality, a prostate cancer awareness initiative, games themed around indigenous reconciliation and gay pride, support for homeless people, a motor neurone disease awareness campaign, and fundraising for a child cancer foundation.

The use of sport to transmit social justice messages went to another level in 2016 when former American National Football League San Francisco 49ers quarterback Colin Kaepernick 'took a knee' instead of standing up as the National Anthem was played before a game. He did this in protest against racism and police brutality across the United States.[35] Kaepernick reportedly said he was 'not going to stand up to show pride in a flag for a country that oppresses black people and people of colour.' Kaepernick's actions created a ripple effect across the American nation, and in 2020, the Milwaukee Bucks – a leading US National Basketball League team – boycotted a game during their playoff series against the Orlando Magic by refusing to come out of their locker room. The boycott was part of a protest that followed from the police shooting of a young African American male. Subsequently, the two other NBA playoff games were postponed. This was followed by the postponement of three women's NBA games, three Major League Baseball games, and five Major League Soccer games, all of which were used to express concerns over racial equality and police violence in the USA.[36] The use of sport to promote social justice issues quickly spread to Europe, and during the 2021 and 2022 European (soccer) football Championships, both England's men's and women's teams 'took the knee.'[37]

The 'taking the knee' social justice movement, which appeared to legitimise the role of the 'activist-athlete'[38] spread to the southern hemisphere. In October 2022, members of the Australian (soccer) football World Cup squad – the Socceroos – got on the social cause bandwagon by releasing a video that called on Qatar's political authorities to improve on its human rights record. The first call was to decriminalise same-sex relationships, and the second was to improve the conditions of Qatar's migrant workers by establishing a migrant resource centre as a legacy of the tournament. Team members conceded that while they were 'not experts,' they had conscientiously listened to the concerns expressed by several authoritative human rights bodies, including Amnesty International, the International Labour Organisation, FIFPRO (the international football players union), and migrant worker representatives based in Qatar. Football Australia, the national governing body for Australian football, also made its presence felt by noting that while 'significant progress and legislative reforms' had taken place in Qatar over recent times, it 'hoped the assurances given by Qatar's Emir, HH Sheikh Tamim Bin Hamad al-Thani, and FIFA president Gianni Infantino' would guarantee 'the safety of LGBTQI+ people … beyond the tournament.'[39]

In the meantime, a 'One Love' campaign had been initiated by the Dutch Football Association to not only 'express their support for unification of all people' but also condemn all forms of discrimination. In September 2022, it was announced that numerous European nations would adopt the campaign, which would include protests during the World Cup. Seven European teams, including the Netherlands and Germany, had planned to wear One-Love armbands as a rebuke to Qatar's laws against homosexuality as well as its treatment of migrant workers during the massive infrastructure build in the lead-up to the big event.[40]

The attacks on Qatar's human rights record reached their zenith during the first week of the World Cup in Qatar, where sporting issues took a back seat to a raft of political messaging. FIFA had just withdrawn its support for the One-Love armband protest, having threatened to book players who wore anything that had the words 'One Love' or 'No Discrimination' on it.[41] But the German team was not deterred. So, as an alternative form of protest, the players decided to cover their mouths for the team photo ahead of their match against Japan. The Dutch, who had championed the initiative in the first place, did not follow the German lead. A player representative subsequently announced that players did not do anything on the field because they felt they had already done enough after meeting some migrant workers directly.[42] Germany was not only left stranded politically speaking, but also lost the game to Japan in a major upset.

In addition, at the beginning of the game between Iran and England, Iran's players stood silent as the nation's national anthem was played. This defiant act was done in support of protests back home over the death of a young woman after being detained by Iran's morality police for apparently not abiding by the country's conservative dress code. A few fans had also protested, with one waving a 'pair of giant scissors' to symbolise the oppression suffered by Iranian women who dared to disobey local laws and clerical demands.[43] It didn't end there. In the lead-up to a subsequent game against the US team, Iranian authorities apparently threatened families of the Iranian players with 'violence and torture' if the players did not 'behave' (that is, failed to smile and sing their national anthem with sufficient gusto). As it turned out, they did as they were told.[44]

Most of these initiatives and incidents were based on a strong moral belief in making society a better place and were thus done for ethical reasons. Nevertheless, the use of sport to communicate socio-political messages in the name of social justice raises many questions. From our perspective, the main one is this: has the social messaging that sport increasingly undertakes in the name of social justice had any lasting impact on its core stakeholders? That is, has it achieved all that it aimed to do with respect to (1) increasing societal awareness of pressing social issues and injustices and (2) changing social attitudes in the ways that were intended?

Our initial response is yes to (1) and no to (2). There is no doubt that sport is a superb conduit for transmitting social marketing and social justice messages. The level of awareness is usually very high, and a lot of media attention follows on from the messaging.[45] However, the studies we reviewed suggest that most of the attitudes and behaviours of people who engage with the world of sport are no less troublesome now than they were in the past. So, while sport has actively pursued a social-justice capital-building agenda over the last 20 years or so, most of it has been ineffectual in driving sizeable or lasting social change outside the sporting bodies themselves, with the 2022 Qatar World Cup protests being a case in point. When the competition got underway, social justice issues were quickly replaced by a plethora of visitor complaints about ticketing mismanagement, alcohol bans, and inconsistent team performances. And, of course, there was the usual complaining about referee ineptitude.

Capital Gaps

It is difficult to include every segment of a society's stocks of capital that sport may have contributed to, or worse, diminished. Natural capital was one of them. The term 'natural capital' was 'coined' in 1973 by E.F. Schumacher in his best-selling book, *Small Is Beautiful,* and since then has found a niche within the field of ecological economics.[46] It is usually defined as the stocks of renewable and non-renewable assets – including soils, forests, water bodies, and all additional flora and fauna – that yield a flow of value-adding ecosystem goods or services into the future. Currently there are vigorous debates about what sport has or has not done to society's stocks of natural capital. Terms like sustainable sport, regenerative sport, and green sport are being thrown around with abandon, but instead of conflating the issues into digestible policy analysis themes, they have revealed a multitude of factors to be addressed and cases to be explored.[47]

Studies based on environmental evidence are largely absent, and the scant few that do are based on short-term observations, although there are books – mainly commentaries wielding generic climate change data – on the topic.[48] We used the same type of argument in deciding to not include an analysis of sport and political capital and its use as a tool of diplomacy.[49] There are major disputes about sport's ability to make the world a more peaceful place. International sports scholar John Hoberman – having examined the peace-making capability of the International Olympic Committee (IOC) and the Fédération de Football Association (FIFA) – found that they could best be described as 'enterprise zones for … compromised and self-serving people who… recruited themselves into national and international sports federations to achieve an international visibility.' According to Hoberman they were essentially 'forms of show business internationalism,' and as far away from 'legitimate international humanitarian organizations such as the Red Cross and Amnesty International' as you could get.[50] In the end, the big problem is the lack of empirical studies upon which to draw an informed position.

Declaring Capital

Having reassembled the claims and counter claims about sport's ability to make society a better place, we are now able to assess its impact more succinctly on the capital accumulation process and the extent to which it confirmed our public value analysis. Table 6.1 tells the story, which is, like our discussion in Chapter 5, not all good. Whatever way you look at it, sport has frequently failed to deliver on its mythical promises while also falling short of community expectations.

Table 6.1 Sport's Capital-Building Impact

Type of capital	*Evidence that sport helps build society's stocks of capital*	*Evidence that sport strips society of its stocks of capital*
Interpersonal	High	Minimal
Economic	Moderate	Low
Educational/ cultural	Moderate	Minimal
Psychological	High	Moderate
Moral	Low	High
Physical	High	Low
Civic	Moderate	Low
Protective	Low	High
Social justice	Moderate	Low

While sport offers multiple spaces for people to meet and make friends and helps attend to the psychological and physical health of its citizens, especially adolescents and young adults, there are currently two major weaknesses and one unfulfilled promise. First, sport has done little to build the moral competencies of its participants, and second (and worst of all), it has progressively undermined its capacity to provide safe spaces for participant engagement. As far as the social justice issue is concerned, the jury is still out. While sporting bodies and many players have both justifiably and enthusiastically taken on social justice causes, there is little evidence that it has had much success in changing social attitudes in the process.

More or Less Capital?

Literally billions of people around the world derive significant meaning from sport, ranging from a contribution to their identity to a reason for living. These direct benefits are incontrovertible. However, when it comes to validating all those additional benefits that are supposed to flow from the sporting experience – the indirect benefits – most of them are found wanting.

There is agreement amongst researchers that sport's capacity to deliver social capital is second to none. Physical capital is, for the most part, enhanced when lots of people spend time on the sports field and the indoor court. There is also enough evidence around to say that economic capital and sport development grow together, although the scale is not often as great as tends to be claimed.[51] Psychological capital can also accumulate with an increase in sport participation, but it can be stripped away when stress and anxiety get out of control. Educational/cultural capital sits someone in the middle. Sport participation can help boys get higher grades, but for most girls it makes little difference. When it comes to civic capital, it is much the same as it is for education and learning. Some participants may secure a benefit, and others not so much, depending on the quality of the programme they have enlisted in. Sport's capacity to build moral capital is clearly negligible. In fact, in many instances it delivers what we might call moral decadence. Sport's ability to deliver protective capital is equally dubious. In fact, we will go so far as to say that, on balance, sport engagement does the opposite. For the most part it does not provide safe spaces for its participants. This seems to be an extreme position to take, but the evidence is strong. On reflection, though, this should not be surprising given that one of sport's great attractions is the risks it evokes. Finally, we have the claim that sport can help build a society's social justice capital. Sport has certainly secured an image as a socially responsible institution that puts fairness, equity, and inclusiveness at the front of its mission statements. Yet there are also critics who believe its social justice campaigns are little more than marketing tactics to secure not only a positive public image or diplomatic 'soft power' but also attract additional sponsors, especially those who want to demonstrate their progressive ethical and political credentials.[52]

Whatever way you look at it (through the public value lens or the capital accumulation lens), sport, as it currently stands, has failed to deliver on many, if not most, of its promises to make society a better place. Moreover, it has done little to reduce the physical, social, and psychological costs that its practice delivers. It wouldn't be unreasonable to assert that sport is facing a crisis of confidence. For every celebration, there is a scandal. If sport is allowed to continue in this mode, then it does not take a genius to conclude that sport is slowly undermining the quality of life and well-being of the citizens who play it and the communities that host it. The question is: what can we do about this serious social problem, which appears to be going from bad to worse?

Notes

1 Pierre Bourdieu (1986). The forms of capital, in J.G. Richardson (ed.), in *Handbook of Theory and Research for the Sociology of Education*, Greenwood Press: 41.

2 Pierre Bourdieu (1979). *Distinction: A Social Critique of the Judgement of Taste*, Harvard University Press. If you want to see how Bourdieu's model of cultural capital and its distribution across society was applied to a non-European setting, you can do no better than taking a look at Tony Bennett, Michael Emmison, and John Frow (1999). *Accounting for Taste: Australian Everyday Cultures*, Cambridge University Press; and Tony Bennett, David Carter, Modesto Gayo, Michelle Kelly, and Greg Noble [eds] (2021). *Fields, Capitals, Habitus: Australian Culture, Inequalities and Social Divisions*, Routledge.

3 Robert Putnam (2000). *Bowling Alone: The Collapse and Revival of American Community*, Simon & Schuster.

4 For a highly informative if somewhat esoteric explanation of human and intellectual, how they can be accumulated, and why they matter, see Kwee Keong (2008). Intellectual capital: Definitions, categorization and reporting models, *Journal of Intellectual Capital*, 9 (4): 609–638

5 It is a term that comes out of the positive psychology movement and supported by the conceptual pillars of hope, efficacy, resilience, and optimism, which are

encapsulated in the acronym HERO. For more details, see Mustafa Fedai Çavuş and Ayşe Gökçen (2015). Psychological capital: Definition, components and effects, *British Journal of Education, Society & Behavioural Science,* 5 (3): 244–255.

6 See Marci Cottingham (2016). Theorizing emotional capital, *Theory and Society,* 45: 451–470.

7 This is the 'stock of the earth's renewable and non-renewable resources, including trees, soils, air, water, and all living things.' For more details, see Scott Mesley, Carolin Leeshaa, and Georgie Aley (2021). *Demystifying Natural Capital and Biodiversity,* KPMG.

8 The idea of spiritual capital was comprehensively examined by David Palmer and Michele Wong (2013). Clarifying the concept of spiritual capital, *Conference on the Social Scientific Study of Religion,* The Chinese University of Hong Kong, 10–13 July.

9 Carola Hommerich and Tim Tiefenbach (2018). Analyzing the relationship between social capital and subjective well-being: The mediating role of social affiliation, *Journal of Happiness Studies,* 19: 1091–1114.

10 Vilius Semenas (2014). Ethnic diversity and social capital at the community level: Effects and implications for policymakers, *Inquiries,* 6 (4). Online publication.

11 For a summary of the contribution sport makes to the economies of Europe, see John Considine (2020). *Economic Impact of Sport in the EU,* Sport Economics, 18 March. Economics of Sport - The Economics of Sport (sportseconomics.org). Considine reported that sport's annual contributions varied from just under 2% for Ireland to just under 5% for Austria.

12 For an excellent explanation of how intellectual capital contributes to economic growth and national well-being, see Organisation for Economic Co-operation and Development (2004). *Creating Value from Intellectual Assets: Meeting of the OECD Council at Ministerial Level. Creating Value from Intellectual Assets (oecd.org).*

13 Rosemary Purcell, Kate Gwyther, and Simon Rice (2019). Mental health in elite athletes: Increased awareness requires an early intervention framework to respond to athlete needs, *Sports Medicine – Open,* 5 (46). Online publication.

14 Frédéric Brière Gabrielle Yale-Soulière, Daniela Gonzalez-Sicilia, Marie-Josée Harbec, Julien Morizot, Michel Janosz, and Linda S. Pagani (2018). Prospective associations between sport participation and psychological adjustment in adolescents, *Journal of Epidemiology and Community Health,* 14 March. Online publication.

15 Our inspiration for using the term 'morally virtuous' came from a re-reading of Jonathan Haidt (2013). *The Righteous Mind: Why Good People Are Divided by Politics and Religion,* Knopf Doubleday: 336–343.

16 Maria Kavussanu and Ali Al-Yaaribi (2021). Prosocial and antisocial behaviour in sport, *International Journal of Sport and Exercise Psychology,* 19 (2): 179–202. Table 1 on p. 181 paints a disheartening picture of the social harms sport can perpetrate on its participants.

17 These factors were highlighted in Beatričė Sipavičiūtė and Saulius Šukys (2019). Understanding factors related with cheating in sport: What we know and what is worth future consideration, *Baltic Journal of Sport & Health Sciences,* 4 (115): 37–45.

18 Again, Pierre Bourdieu was instrumental in getting this concept off the ground, although he preferred the term 'bodily capital.' See, for example, Pierre Bourdieu (1978). Sport and Social Class. *Social Science Information,* 17(6): 819–840. It has gone through a few updates since then and now incorporates the investment people make in time, money, and energy into their bodies – including cosmetic surgery, makeovers, exercise, dieting, clothing choices, hairstyle, and tattoos – and what they expect to receive in return. Our emphasis in is on health, fitness, and appearance.

19 Jung Ha Park, Ji Hyun Moon, Hyeon Ju Kim, Mi Hee Kong, and Yun Hwan Oh (2019). Sedentary lifestyle: Overview of updated evidence of potential health risks sedentary lifestyle, *Korean Journal of Family Medicine,* 41 (6): 365–373.

20 Ciaran O'Neill, Helen McAneney, Frank Kee, and Mark Tully (2017). Direct healthcare costs of sedentary behaviour in the UK, *Journal of Epidemiology and Community Health*, 73: 7. Online publication.

21 There is general agreement that civic capital is driven by community engagement activities where citizens contribute to programmes that aim to improve the quality of life and overall level of well-being. The focus of attention is usually a disadvantaged group or issue of public concern, including homelessness, pollution, food insecurity, and people with disabilities. It can also cover volunteer work for not-for-profit organisations, including social welfare agencies and, of course, sporting organisations. For a detailed analyst of civic engagement and its capital-building capacity, see Richard Adler and Judy Goggin (2005). What do we mean by "civic engagement?" *Journal of Transformative Education,* 3 (3): 236–253.

22 See, for example, Tim Pawlowski, Paul Downward, and Simona Rasciute (2014). Does national pride from international sporting success contribute to well-being? An international investigation, *Sport Management Review,* 17(2): 121–132. If you want to understand how civic pride works at a more generic level, there is a lot to be learned by reading Tom Collins (2016). Urban civic pride and the new localism, *Transactions of the Institute of British Geographers*, 41 (2): 175–186.

23 We adapted this theme from the world of accounting and finance, where a lot is said about the ways in which asset values can be safely protected, and the risk of losses lowered. The concept of 'protected investment' has been used to explain the importance of mitigating risk and ensuring the gains are not stripped away by harmful incidents. So, in the context our study, protective capital comprises all those provisions protocols, safeguards, and rules that preserve the benefits and value that accrues from sport engagement.

24 An excellent overview of sport and risk from an athlete's perspective is available in Michael Atkinson (2019). Sport and risk culture: The suffering body in sport, *Research in the Sociology of Sport*, 12: 5–21.

25 In Australia, the sports rumour mill was rife with allegations of sexual abuse in elite swimming. It got comprehensively exposed in 2015 when the Royal Commission into Institutional Responses to Child Sexual completed a swimming case study. The details are laid out in the *Report of Case Study Number 15 (2015). Response of swimming institutions, the Queensland and NSW Offices of the DPP and the Queensland Commission for Children and Young People and Child Guardian to Allegations of Child Sexual Abuse by Swimming Coaches*, November. But that was only the beginning. In 2021, a commissioned report found that sexual abuse was endemic in competitive swimming with nearly all of it being perpetrated by coaches.

26 See, for example, Australian Human Rights Commission (2021). *Change the Routine: Report on the Independent Review into Gymnastics in Australia*, Australian Government. On page 9, it stated that a 'win-at-all-costs' culture that prevailed across the sport had 'created unacceptable risks for the safety and wellbeing of often very young gymnasts.' And the situation was even worse in the United States, where, in 2017, Larry Nassar, the former team doctor for the national gymnastics squad, pleaded guilty in a Michigan court to having sexually abused 10 minors in addition to more than 100 older gymnasts under his care. He was given a life sentence.

27 In December 2020, the US Government Accountability Office released a report on athlete safety. It painted an horrific picture. It was titled *Amateur Athletes: The U.S. Center for SafeSport's Response and Resolution Process for Reporting Abuse.*

In 2019, the Center – which was established in the wake of the Larry Nasser Scandal - received about 2400 incidents of sexual assault and/or abuse.

28 David Maume and Michael Parrish (2021). Heavy-contact sport participation and early adolescent delinquency, *Social Currents*, 8 (2): 126–144.

29 We took social justice to mean a critical desire to eliminate all inequalities and disadvantage in society by redistributing incomes, removing discriminatory practices, and protecting the rights of all individuals no matter what their background, role, or status. For a full explanation of what social justice means you can do no better than read Allan Ornstein (2017). Social justice: History, purpose and meaning, *Social Science and Public Policy*, 54: 541–548. For something that offers a more theoretical explanation of social justice, we suggest you go to Emil Dinga (2014). Social capital and social justice: Economic scientific research - Theoretical, empirical and practical approaches, *Procedia Economics and Finance,* 8: 246–253.

30 George Cunningham (2015). LGBT inclusive athletic departments as agents of social change, *Journal of Intercollegiate Sport*, 8: 43–56.

31 In 2020, a book devoted entirely to social justice issues in sport was published under the Routledge banner. It was edited by Nick Watson, Grant Jarvie, and Andrew Parker and titled *Sport, Physical Education, and Social Justice: Religious, Sociological, Psychological, and Capability Perspectives*. According to the publisher's 'blurb,' the book 'demonstrates the multiple ways in which sport can be used to overcome inequalities and marginalisation relating to gender, race, disability, religion, and sexuality.' It also positioned sports education as a mechanism for addressing school-based issues including bullying, racism, and citizenship education.

32 Talent Moyo, Rodney Duffett, and Brendon Knott (2022). An analysis of cause-related and social marketing strategies in the south African sport management industry, *SAGE Open:* Online. April. See also Jennifer Pharr and Nancy Lough (2015). Differentiation of social marketing and cause-related marketing in US professional sport, *Sport Marketing Quarterly*, 21: 91–903.

33 Veteran American sport journalist, Robert Scoop Jackson, also reminded us that that 'sport, historically, has been a pulpit for protest.' He cited the exploits of African American prize-fighter, Jack Johnson, who, in 1908, took on Tommy Burns. In front of thousands of spectators in Sydney, Australia, Johnson defeated Burns, and thus became the first black heavyweight champion of the world. Johnson held the crown for seven more years. Despite the rampant racial animosity, segregation, and occasional lynching during this period, Jack regularly spoke out against white supremacy and American racism. For details, see Robert Scoop Jackson (2020). *The Game is Not a Game: The Power, Protests and Politics of American Sports*, Haymarket Books: 198–200.

34 This point was succinctly highlighted in Ronald Woods and Nalani Butler (2021). *Social Issues in Sport - fourth edition*, Human Kinetics: 347–351.

35 The action of kneeling dated back to the civil rights movement in the United States, where nationally known figures such as Martin Luther King kneeled after leading a prayer as protesters were arrested during a 1965 march to the USA Dallas County (Alabama) courthouse.

36 Chris Bengel (2020). Sports protests: A look at how athletes have boycotted for social justice throughout history. *CBS Sports,* 27 August.

37 Staff Reporter (2022). What's taking the knee and why is it important? *BBC News* 22 November.

38 Ryan Broussar (2020). 'Stick to sports' is gone: A field theory analysis of sports journalists' coverage of socio-political issues, *Journalism Studies*, 21 (12): 1627–1643.

39 Tracey Holmes (2022). Socceroos call on Qatar to decriminalise same-sex relationships on eve of FIFA World Cup, *ABC News – The Ticket*, 27 October.

40 Armani Syed (2022). The 'one love' LGBTQ rights armband is causing a stir at the Qatar World Cup, *Time*, 21 November.

41 Ian Ladyman (2022.) Kane reveals he was disappointed not to wear 'one love' armband, *The Daily Mail*, 22 November.
42 The Associated Press (2022). Dutch not expected to emulate Germany with World Cup protest, *ABC News,* November 25. Dutch not expected to emulate Germany with World Cup protest - ABC News (go.com)
43 Ben Church (2022). Iran players remain silent during national anthem at World Cup in Apparent Protest at Iranian Regime, *CNN Sport*, 21 November.
44 Daniel Chavkin (2022). Iran threatens to torture players' families ahead of USMNT match, *Sports Illustrated,* 29 November.
45 Hesham Zafar (2021). How the power of sport can bring us together and drive social justice, *World Economic Forum*, 8 January. How sports can bring us together and drive social justice | World Economic Forum (weforum.org)
46 The seminal article in this field study was Robert Costanza and Herman Daly (1992). Natural capital and sustainable development, *Conservation Biology*, 6 (1): 37–46.
47 For a comprehensive overview of the sport, natural capital, and sustainability issue, see Hallgeir Gammelsæter and Sigmund Loland (2023). Code red for elite sport. A critique of sustainability in elite sport and a tentative reform programme, *European Sport Management Quarterly*, 23 (1): 104–124. The authors concluded that neither sport's governing bodies, governments, nor the sport industry were 'currently enforcing effective measures to transform elite sport into an activity that contributes to global cooling.' But they also said that things could be improved if sporting bodies first, reduced their long-distance travel arrangements, second, lowered the use and construction of infrastructure and facilities, third, limited the use and promotion of fast fashion and sporting equipment, and fourth, ensured that sports mega-events no longer be admitted as economic guarantees or tax exemption in the belief that such events were 'an effective way of enhancing public welfare.' For a detailed discussion on soccer-football and sustainability, see Leslie Mabon (2023). Football and climate change: What do we know, and what is needed for an evidence-informed response? *Climate Policy*, 23 (3): 314–328.
48 As it turns out, a first go has been made, which is Stavros Triantafyllidis and Cheryl Mallen (2022*). Sport and Sustainable Development: An Introduction*, Routledge.
49 An illuminating introduction to the sport diplomacy field of study is contained in Philippe Vonnard and Kevin Marston (2020). Playing across the 'Halfway Line' on the fields of international relations: The journey from globalising sport to sport diplomacy, *Contemporary European History*, 29 (2): 220–231.
50 John Hoberman (2011). The myth of sport as a peace-promoting political force, *SAIS Review Peace-Provol.* XXXI (1): 17–29.
51 Caution is needed when examining data that purport to show the extent to which sport investment (be it infrastructure or participant spending) has impacted on total economic activity. Take, for example, a 2018 study into the economic impact of sport on the Australian economy. It began by stating that the initial national annual spend on sport was $6 billion. It went on to calculate the multiplier effect which was the additional income spending that followed on from the initial direct spend. The multiplier had two parts. Part one was the indirect effect which accounted for the additional spending by suppliers to the sport sector. This came in at $5 billion. Part two was the induced effect which accounted for the additional spending by employees in the sport sector. This came in at $28 billion. This meant the initial $6 billion spend had an overall economic impact of $39 billion. This gave us a multiplier of just over 6, which said that for every $1 spent, the aggregated economic gain was around $6. This is a mightily impressive figure since multipliers of 2 are the norm. For all the details of this study, see The Boston Consulting group (2017). *Intergenerational Review of Australian Sport*, Australian Government / Australian Sports Commission: 42–43. And further caution is required when dealing with the

economic value of sports volunteering. In some instances, volunteering is treated as a benefit since it adds value, but in other situations, it is viewed as a spend (or cost, if you like), since it uses up the scare spare-time of participants. For an example of how volunteerism is treated as a benefit, see KPMG (2018). *Investigating the Value of Community Sport Infrastructure in Australia, Investigating the Value of Community Sport facilities in Australia,* Australian Government / Australian Sports Commission: 12.

52 The term 'sportswashing' – which often goes under the generic heading of 'reputational laundering' – was invented to describe this practice. It refers to situations where individuals, groups, corporations, or governments use their links to a socially progressive entity, be it a sporting body, event, or some fashionable – or indeed, crucially important – social cause, to rehabilitate a reputation tarnished by a prior wrongdoing. For a commercial business, sportswashing can be undertaken by hosting big sport events, partnering up with a sports league, sponsoring a team, or underwriting a community physical activity campaign. It can also be used by national governments as a propaganda and soft-diplomacy tool to direct attention away from poor human rights records, corruption scandals, and international criminal allegations. In the case of a sporting body, sportswashing can be undertaken by partnering up with a gender equity campaign, a male violence counselling body, an anti-homophobia agency, an anti-gambling authority, or an environmental protection group. An excellent overview of sports washing can be found in Michael Skey (2022). Sportswashing: Media headline or analytic concept? *International Review for the Sociology of Sport*, 1–16. Online publication. Skey also situated sportswashing in the context of other forms of 'washing' including whitewashing, greenwashing, pink-washing, and even vegan-washing. If you want to dive even deeper into the sportswashing pool, you should also read Kyle Fruh, Alfred Archer, and Jake Wojtowicz (2022). Sportswashing: Complicity and corruption, *Sport, Ethics and Philosophy*, 17 (1): 101–118. The authors examined the sportswashing issue in the context of international football/soccer.

7 The Problem with Sport

What's the Problem?

Having interrogated the claims made in support of sport's ability to make the world a better place, how successful has it been in achieving its lofty goal? The previous chapters delivered a lot of good stories about sport's place in society. We found that it was embedded in the culture and economy of nearly every nation on this planet. It occupied people's spare time in many positive ways. It brought people together, it got its citizens fitter and healthier than they might otherwise have been, and it took them into spaces where they could momentarily forget about both the banalities and stresses of everyday life.

Sport also had deeper experiences to offer. It took its followers back to the tribal ways of hunter-gatherers, where physical prowess was celebrated, and contests were used to hone the skills of would-be warriors. Sporting heroes were lauded and given God-like status through their inclusion in religious ceremonies.

But that was only the beginning. Sport also evolved into a form of entertainment, and by the end of the 20th century had become an industry that not only delivered huge at-ground attendances but also had a massive media presence. While only 10–15% of citizens in western industrialised nations engaged with sport as players or participants, around 70% of adults had an interest in it, a majority of whom watch it on television.[1]

We also found out that not all sports had mass appeal. Team sports – especially those that included some form of body contact, with the football codes front and centre – attracted huge audiences while also securing most of the media reporting. On the other hand, individual sports where participants had little direct contact – with archery, shooting, and diving being prime examples – mostly languished when it came to spectator support.

These findings provided a backdrop to the thrust of our diagnosis, which was to strip sport bare and reveal its true nature as opposed to its mythological appearance.

DOI: 10.4324/9781003546931-7

Public Value Revisited

To put it as sharply as we can, once we removed the direct intrinsic pleasure people get from doing sport, we found that sport's supposed ability to deliver a whole raft of indirect benefits was massively overrated. As we showed, most of its public value propositions (PVPs) had failed to deliver on their promises. Here's a summary:

1. While sport participation can, in many circumstances, help adolescents – especially boys – improve their scholastic capability, it does not, of itself, make young people smarter and more knowledgeable.
2. Sport engagement can assist young people to act responsibly and build their confidence, but the assertion that it turns callow youths into civic-minded adults ready to lead others has only limited supporting evidence.
3. The argument that sport engagement makes its participants morally virtuous by having them deal with conflicted choices has no supporting evidence. If anything, the opposite is the case.
4. The claim that sport participants have more friends than those who did not engage with sport has a lot going for it. But it is equally true that sport can sometimes erect barriers to building friendships across different demographic and cultural groupings and can tend to be exclusive rather than inclusive.
5. While it makes intuitive sense to believe that the sporting achievements of elite athletes create positive role models for emulation by young people, there is next to no supporting evidence. In fact, the available evidence suggests that many elite athletes are not particularly good role models at all, and what is more, there isn't much evidence that elite athletes who are worth emulating have any positive effect on deliver moments of joy and periods of happiness, the behaviours of young people either.
6. Sport engagement has the potential to lower the incidence of juvenile crime, but it only works in highly organised interventions backed by professional expertise and social support programmes.
7. Sport participation does, in the main, deliver moments of joy and periods of happiness, but it rarely fulfils the grand ambitions and heroic dreams of many of its followers.
8. The claim that sport enables people to live healthier and longer lives with fewer disabilities is, for the most part, true, but it hides the fact that regular physical activity can deliver similar benefits at a lower cost.
9. There is growing evidence that sport engagement protects some, but not all, participants from long-term psychological harm, but it can also create additional stress and anxiety.
10. The idea that sport is a safety valve for the release of pent-up aggression and hostility has made intuitive sense for a long time, but the evidence

says that in many circumstances it leads to even more aggressive and hostile behaviour.

11 It is true that sport might enable its participants to build work-ready capabilities that result in high-wage jobs, but there are still disputes about the causal nature of this relationship.
12 There is evidence that sport contributes to the growth of local economies by attracting infrastructure, visitor expenditure, and more jobs. But the scale of the effect is lowered considerably when government subsidies, community assistance, corporate partnerships, and the takeover of local facilities are accounted for. Nor does it account for the opportunity costs of the same investment elsewhere.
13 While sport has become a conduit of choice for promoting social causes and progressive beliefs, there is little evidence to show that it has a significant impact on social attitudes and behaviour in society.
14 While sport provides places for fans to become positively active members of intimately engaged communities, it can also provide spaces for all sorts of misogynistic, homophobic, racist, and crazy conspiratorial rants.
15 The claim that sport provides safe and protective spaces for securing exhilarating experiences is completely unfounded. There is growing evidence that the risks associated with some types of sport engagement are so high that you are left wondering why they receive so much corporate and government support.

Capital Accumulation Re-tested

Our initial response to the above findings was to think we had been too selective with our case analysis and had let our biases contaminate their conclusions. As a result, we decided to do a 'cross-check' by looking at things through another conceptual lens. So, this time we ditched the PVP model and adopted a capital formation/accumulation approach, which we used to examine the ways sport might either add to or reduce a society's stocks of capital (its physical and human assets, if you like). Our findings were remarkably like our public value results. That is, while sport engagement delivered significant increases to society's stocks of capital, there were many instances where it depleted it. We found that:

1 Sport can build what we called **interpersonal capital** by bringing people together in the neighbourhood, the local community, and the nation. It enables people to assimilate into social groups by providing safe spaces for light conversation, harmless banter, and even serious debate. But there was also a tendency for people to congregate with those who look, think, and act in similar ways to themselves.

2 Society's stocks of **economic capital** can be enhanced at both the individual and community levels. People who play sport at school earn more than non-participants when in the workforce, while sport events can stimulate local economies. However, the impact can be exaggerated by generous government and community support, and it does not last for long in most situations.
3 On balance, sport participation will add to the stocks of **educational and cultural capital**, since many students – but mainly boys – who play sport achieve better academic results than those who did not. But it was not clear that sport was the direct cause of the difference. Greater self-discipline and a more positive attitude to school in general may have been contributing factors.
4 When it comes to **psychological capital**, children and adolescents who are exposed to well-administered sports programmes had a greater chance of becoming relatively well-adjusted adults. But, overall, sport participation is not a panacea for unhappiness, low self-esteem, emotional fragility, chronic stress, anxiety, or depression. In hyper-competitive settings, psychological capital can be stripped away by public humiliation and trauma.
5 Sport can inflict massive moral harm on its participants, especially when the desire to win becomes obsessive. And there is no support for the claim that role models had any lasting positive influence on impressionable children and adolescents. In short, sport – no matter what the level of competition – can deplete society's stocks of **moral capital**.
6 There is furious agreement that sport participation had a positive effect on health and longevity, but there are also many examples where society's stocks of **physical capital** can be eroded, since in many instances participants are more likely to use smokeless tobacco, binge drink, and have disordered eating than non-participants.
7 When it came to **civic capital**, there were signs that people who played sport – especially as adolescents – were more engaged in community affairs, clubs, and associations than those who did not. But there were also some instances where young adult males who were heavily involved in high-contact team sports were less likely to contribute to the life of their local communities by doing good and making a difference.
8 It was nearly all one way when it came to sport's contribution to a society's stocks of **protective capital**. But disappointingly, the effect was negative. The research showed increased participation in heavy contact sports not only led to more serious on-field injuries – with concussions an escalating problem – but was also associated with increased levels of violent and property crimes in early adolescence. In addition, gambling became addictive amongst many sport followers, with racism embedded in the sporting landscape, homophobia bubbling just beneath the surface, and misogyny and sexism occupying nearly every nook and cranny of locker

rooms. Instead of building up society's protective capital, sport was stripping it away at every turn.

9 At first glance, it appears that sport, particularly over the past decade or so, had made an exponentially increasing contribution to society's stocks of **social justice capital**. It had effectively become a 'champion' of social justice by taking up a plethora of socio-political – often called 'social cause' or 'social justice' – messages. However, there was little evidence to indicate that it changed social values, beliefs, and attitudes for the better.

Is Sport Failing Its Citizens and Communities?

As far as we are concerned, these findings are abundantly clear. Sport can no longer pretend to possess the unique capability of making everything it touches turn to economic, social, and cultural gold. Yes, it engages millions of people across the planet, it takes up a lot of their leisure time, it keeps them active, and it makes them happy most of the time. However, it also has a disturbing propensity to not only fail to deliver the social goods it claims to, but also cause an enormous amount of harm. This very point was addressed in 2021 by the *Centre for Sport and Human Rights*, located in Geneva, Switzerland. It noted that while the 'foundational principles of the world's preeminent sports bodies speak to universal humanitarian values, harmony among nations, solidarity and fair play, the preservation of human dignity, and commitment to non-discrimination,' the fact of the matter is that human rights violations have grown exponentially. It cited cases of mental, physical, and sexual abuse and harassment; gender discrimination; racist and homophobic abuse; and the unlawful detention of athletes protesting over 'political regimes in their countries.'[2] It went on to say that the United Nations Guiding Principles on Business and Human Rights (UNGPs) have been acknowledged as 'the authoritative framework and roadmap for sport governing bodies (SGBs) on human rights.'[3] Progress has been slow, with some SGBs unwilling to adopt international human rights norms and standards, having argued that UNGPs are non-binding and apply only to commercial enterprises.

We take the side of the *Centre for Sport and Human Rights*. Sport's ability to increase public value and build society's stocks of capital will spiral downward so long as sport administrators, government officials, and media commentators believe all the myths that surround the theory and practice of sport while viewing the costs as low-grade collateral damage. Moreover, sport's capacity to do good things for society will continue to decline until the government takes a hard look at the reality of sport and works out what additional policies will be needed to maintain its reputation for social improvement and making the world a better place. Otherwise, sport may end up being an overrated institution that creates as much mayhem as it does joy for its participants.

In the light of what we found, it is clear to us that sport has many serious problems to contend with. Many of them are of its own making since it has taken on roles for which it is poorly equipped to handle. The belief that sport can act as a rite of passage for adolescents (where character is formed and morality developed) is a case in point. Other problems are built into the very essence of sport, with competition and the often obsessive need to defeat one's opponent being preeminent. So too is the massive popularity of collision team sports, where the likelihood of injury is high, and the philosophy of hurting your opponents is not discouraged.

This begs the obvious question: what needs to be done to make sure sport will build more public value and societal capital while minimising the ever-increasing risks and harms that make it such a costly enterprise? Before we answer this question, we should be clear about what problems need to be addressed and what 'roadblocks' need to be removed to ensure sport does more good than harm.

Specifying the Problems

As we have noted, sport has never been so popular and so generously funded by both business and government. As we have also shown, it has never had so many problems to sort out. At every turn, there is something that threatens to undermine its good standing. For instance:

1 Sporting bodies operate under the mistaken assumption that by exposing young people to competitive activities involving physical contests, they can shape their character, morals, and civic sensitivities in positive ways. The evidence says they rarely do.
2 Sporting bodies spend a lot of time and money cultivating heroic qualities in their elite athletes and using them as role models to inspire young people to act with greater social and ethical awareness. They do this not knowing it doesn't work.
3 By having a competitive ethos as their cultural centrepiece, sporting bodies create stressful climates where psychological disorders become common occurrences.
4 Sport's competitive ethos encourages over-training and match-day risk taking, putting enormous strain on the body, culminating in injuries to joints, ligaments, muscles, and, in collision sports, the human brain.
5 The competitive ethos also means that many participants will do all that it takes to win, which means resorting to the use of performance-enhancing substances and other forms of cheating, corruption, or poor conduct.
6 The fact that contests involving high levels of physical contact attract the most participants – with many of them being instinctively aggressive – means that head injuries and concussions have become a major issue for team sports.

7. So long as sporting contests are organised around the principle of 'outcome uncertainty,' they are ideal spaces for gambling.
8. Paradoxically, this desire to create uncertainty plays perfectly into the hands of betting consortiums who are prepared to bribe players to play 'dead,' throw matches and fights, and incentivise referees to favour one team over another.
9. While sport's governing bodies, associations, and clubs have devoted an enormous amount of time and money to make sport a welcoming and inclusive enterprise, the evidence points in the other direction. Racism, misogyny, and homophobia are rampant amongst not only many community clubs but also supporter groups.
10. Sport can deliver its supporters moments of intense joy, but the spectator experience can easily degenerate into moments of personal despair as well as collective madness and extreme violence.
11. Sport makes a big thing of its ability to make people safe, happy, and healthy, especially as they get older, while also providing space for the attainment of personal enrichment and collective enjoyment. But sport can easily become a world of unsafe spaces full of people with massive egos, dubious morals, unbridled ambitions, personality disorders, intolerant prejudices, and predatory inclinations, who contaminate sport's virtues.
12. Paradoxically, sporting entities around the world have used their reputation for ensuring a level playing field – where everyone can be a winner some time in their sporting life – to persuade governments to exclude them from anti-discrimination laws. As a result, they can, where appropriate, discriminate against (that is, exclude) people from a team or competition based on age, disability, sex, and gender identity.

The problems are extensive and formidable, but there are some base-level issues that stand out starkly. Of the 15 public value propositions we interrogated, 12 were exaggerated. Of the nine types of capital formation we examined, only three were positively impacted upon on a regular basis by sport engagement. In some instances, they were little more than romantic myths. But even worse than that, sport had inflicted a vast array of costs and harms on its key stakeholders. They were first its players, second its officials, and finally, those who identified as fans.

If you were unfamiliar with the world of sport and read the above commentary, you would be forgiven for thinking sport is unable to manage its own affairs and is unconstrained by any form of regulation, be it internal rules set by sport's governing bodies or external rules introduced by government. Sport is, in fact, surrounded by a plethora of rules that determine how the game is played, how it is organised, and who may or may not play in one competition but not another. Player behaviour is also regulated by codes of conduct, and something as simple as what can be worn on the court or field of play is often stipulated in eye-catching detail. In the professional side of sport, collective bargaining agreements provide additional constraints on player behaviour, including what they can say and how they should behave in public spaces outside of sport. The safety of players, officials, referees, and spectators is additionally protected by a raft of regulatory instruments, while in recent times sporting bodies have gone beyond the call of duty, so to speak, by taking on social causes that place demands on players and club members for support.

Unfortunately, these rules, regulations, constraints, and restrictions have not always delivered either the societal benefits sport has promised or met society's expectations. There are three reasons for this. First, some regulations have had unfavourable unintended consequences. Second, not all regulations are obeyed, and as a result, the level of compliance is low. Finally, in cases where harm is evident, there has been an absence of appropriate regulation.

Ineffective regulations are not the only reason sport does not always deliver on its promises. The other is a resource issue. Many of the promises that sport makes about making a society a better place are often unfulfilled since they do not have either the physical spaces or intellectual weight to deliver on their aspirations. This leads us to the next question: what needs to be done to ensure that sport delivers on its promises when the evidence suggests it has often failed?

Notes

1 The Tour de France cycle race for men is the most-watched sporting event across the world, with an aggregated viewing audience of around 3.5 billion. The FIFA Men's World Cup is not far behind, with an aggregated audience of just over 3 billion. The total television audience of the Cricket World Cup for men is around 2.6 billion. The English Premier League (EPL) has the highest viewer number over the season, with 4.7 billion people worldwide watching every year. More details can be secured from *2023 Sports Viewership Statistics: How Many People Watch Sports? - Come To Play.*

2 William Rook, Thays Prado, and Daniela Heerdt (2022). Responsible sport: No going back, *The International Sports Law Journal.* https://doi.org/10.1007/s40318-022-00231-4.

3 William Rook, Thays Prado, and Daniela Heerdt (2022). Responsible sport: No going back, *The International Sports Law Journal.* https://doi.org/10.1007/s40318-022-00231-4.

8 The Future of Sport

Regulation Done Well

So, what needs to be done to make sure sport builds more public value and societal capital while minimising the ever-increasing risks and harms that make it costly? We wrapped up the previous chapter by concluding that for all the intrinsic enjoyment sport brings to its followers, it has not only failed to deliver on its additional promises but also initiated a vast array of hurt and harms, which in the business world would be seen as serious 'market failures.'[1] It was hard to fathom how and why this had occurred, since across the planet, sport had been surrounded by a pile of laws, rules, and protocols aimed at keeping it clean, fair, inclusive, and safe.

Sporting organisations have always understood the importance of laws, rules, and protocols and how they could be employed to uphold standards, especially when it came to 'fair play, fair competition, and sportsmanlike [conduct].'[2] But there was also an acknowledgement that many participants sought experiences that were not only fun and inclusive but also risky. Furthermore, a growing number of sport researchers were arguing that sport was prone to market failure because of its adversarial nature, which was embedded in the conduct of both players and spectators, and thus heightened the probability of harm (both intended and inadvertent) occurring.[3] Finally, they were aware that some type of regulation – be it self-determined[4] or externally imposed[5] – was essential in preventing market failures by creating both an ethos (a system of values) and a code of conduct (the rules of engagement) that set the parameters for safe, satisfying, and prolonged participation.[6] It was further clear that both sport governing bodies and governments around the world had taken strong measures to maintain the legitimacy and integrity of sport.[7] Let's consider, then, some examples of how regulation in sport has worked.

We first reflect on the notion of self-regulation and its application to Formula One (F1) motor racing, selected because it provided an excellent example of how an international governing body – in this case, the Fédération Internationale de l'Automobile (FIA) – applied strict regulations that not only controlled and defined the sport but also enhanced its public appeal.

DOI: 10.4324/9781003546931-8

We noticed that the rules were re-jigged nearly every year and, for the most part, prioritised safety while also being adapted to lower the cost of entry for new teams. They had been used to make racing more interesting, where in recent times, rules were adjusted to make 'vehicle overtaking' easier while also preventing one team from securing a major technical advantage over another.[8] Despite the mass of regulations in F1, it was generally agreed that they had benefitted the motor racing community since spectator excitement had been enhanced and the safety of all had been improved.

External regulation takes a different approach. In these instances, governments – through some form of direct oversight – have intervened in sport 'markets' to make sure they worked more efficiently. Boxing, the martial arts, and horse racing were always heavily regulated, and this made a lot of sense given their propensity to cause massive harm in the form of serious injuries, match fixing, and money laundering. Take, for example, the Australian state of New South Wales (NSW), where boxing and the martial art kickboxing are popular combat sports. They were initially regulated under the *Boxing and Wrestling Control Act 1986*, but in response to some structural weaknesses in the governance of the sport, the increasing participation of women, and instances of inept administration, the 1986 act was replaced by the *Combat Sports Act 2013*.[9] Under this new Act, the Boxing Authority of NSW was replaced by the Combat Sports Authority (CSA) of NSW. CSA had an expanded role, which made it responsible for not only the regulation of boxing and wrestling but also Muay Thai (Thai kickboxing), mixed martial arts, and ultimate fighting. Its coverage also included both professional and amateur boxing and women's boxing. The Act set out the requirements for the registration of professional boxers and industry participants, which included promoters, matchmakers, managers, trainers, seconds, referees, judges, and timekeepers. It further determined the conditions under which competitors could compete and events could be staged. Overall, it had the authority to restrict entry into the industry and make participation conditional upon meeting proscribed safety and registration requirements. There was little doubt that without this type of external regulation, the combat sports would have degenerated into a chaotic mix of physical harm, match fixing, and widespread corruption.

Horse racing has also been subject to heavy external regulation for most of its 200-year history,[10] which is not surprising given its capacity to attract 'shady' personalities and incorporate controversial practices in its operations.[11] It crosses social classes,[12] but it is also a high-risk sport, where injury to jockeys and horses are occupational hazards, and its close connections to gambling heighten the potential for corrupt activities to emerge.[13] The regulation of horse racing in Canada is especially strong. Each province has detailed legislation which sets out what horse racing participants could and could not legally do. For example, in British Columbia horse racing is controlled through *the Rules of Thoroughbred and Standardbred Horse Racing*, which was authorised under Section 53 of the *Gaming Control Act and Gaming Control*

Regulation 2002. The rules were both detailed and wide-ranging. They began with the licencing requirements, which covered more than 40 jobs and positions and ranged from owners, trainers, and jockeys to veterinarians, farriers, and track superintendents. They went on to specify the roles of stewards and judges, the responsibilities of veterinarians, procedures for entry nomination and weight allocations, the use of supplements and substances, drug testing regimes, prohibited conduct for participants – which included penalties for being intoxicated, being cruel to horses, and using offensive language – rules for jockeys, handlers, and starters, and finally, the rules for the race itself.

The Australian national government's approach to sport regulation is particularly interesting since it aims to be both collaborative and holistic. Its 2018 sport regulatory strategy, which went under the title of *Safeguarding the Integrity of Sport*, was, on paper, an impressive example of external regulation. Australia's anti-doping regime has also been forcefully managed, having been framed by the heavily punitive World Anti-Doping Agency (WADA) regulations, which became a template for the Australian Sports Anti-Doping Authority (ASADA), which was subsequently recast as Sport Integrity Australia (SIA).

SIA's role was to conduct testing for banned substances, investigate suspected breaches of the regulations, and hand out punishments – mainly in the form of competition bans – where athletes were found to have possessed, trafficked, or used a banned substance. Second, regulations were introduced to counter match fixing and other corrupt behaviour. Third, gambling laws were modified to make gambling operators initiate agreements with the relevant governing bodies on the fee to be paid for utilising the sport's 'competition' as well as the betting protocols. And, in 2020, the Australian government established the National Sports Tribunal, whose role was to resolve sporting disputes within Australia. It was effectively a local version of the Court of Arbitration for Sport, which the International Olympic Committee set up to hear grievances and adjudicate disputes in the international sports arena.

Australia in not alone in establishing rules and guidelines for ensuring a well-managed sporting sector. Around the world, a broad array of regulatory regimes have been put in place to make sure sporting activities were safe, competition was unfettered, cheating was minimised, and corrupt practices were absent.[14] Moreover, these regulatory regimes have usually been quite varied.[15]

Regulation Done Badly

But the fact remains that sporting bodies have not always acted ethically, even when they were subject to an array of regulatory regimes.[16] Sport has suffered from frequent bouts of regulatory failure.[17] Take the case of professional cycling, where its self-regulation processes were left in tatters following the high-profile doping scandal involving Lance Armstrong and many others.

The 2012 revelations severely tested (some would say extinguished) the legitimacy of the international cycling body, Unione Cycliste Internationale (UCI), as the promoter, organiser, and 'policeman' of the sport.[18] In these instances, regulatory failure often led to government enquiries and calls for external intervention.[19] When it comes to external regulation, the World Anti-Doping Agency's anti-doping rules and drug-use protocols have been regularly undermined by bouts of player non-compliance. It has been abundantly clear for some time that something was going horribly wrong.[20]

Similarly, the exponential growth in sports-related injuries and the costs of managing them suggested that the current arrangements for their reduction were not working. It was not just a physical harm problem sport was having to deal with. Additional mental health problems had also been revealed, which, in some cases, seem to be exacerbated under the demands of high-performance sport. Sporting bodies were under more pressure than ever before when it came to balancing the freedom to do exhilarating and risky things against the harms that occurred when the will to win and the need to explore one's limits ended in disaster. There was also all the other stuff around gambling, match-fixing, and corruption that continued to undermine the integrity of sport.[21] When financial and legal issues were added to the mix, sport's governing bodies were faced with a multitude of problems that could only be properly tackled by investing in new policies and strategic initiatives.

Regulatory failures have never sat well with sport's purported selfless mission of serving the community and doing good. The reality was something different, since the will to win, the desire to secure additional power and influence, the need to generate more revenue, and the drive to build strong commercial partnerships – even with businesses whose ethics were questionable – always remained front and centre.[22] We now face an unfortunate reality where, just like the profit-making private sector, the not-for-profit sporting sector cannot always be trusted to responsibly manage its affairs and act in the interests of ordinary citizens.[23]

While there are many examples of sporting bodies doing good things for communities,[24] there are many instances where sport has created all sorts of risks and harms. As a result, society can be stripped of its protective capital by being a catalyst for the expansion of unsafe spaces where injuries are rife,[25] cheating is commonplace,[26] match fixing is endemic,[27] financial mismanagement is rampant,[28] and drug use remains out of control.[29] We have reached the point where no matter what sport's governing bodies do and what governments legislate for, things do not necessarily change for the better.[30] To add to the disappointment, many sport followers not only appeared unworried but also seemed to revel in the furore and the scandals.[31]

As noted in earlier chapters, anti-social spectator behaviour at sporting events has also become a significant social, economic, and cultural problem.[32] It has presented a serious health policy concern in terms of 1) the physical safety of sport spectators, 2) their opportunity to engage with sport and physical activity in a non-discriminatory environment free from racial, cultural, and sexual abuse, and 3) their perceptions, interest, and involvement in sporting participation. For example, soccer-football has been plagued by spectator aggression but was by no means the only sport open to public scrutiny for its 'patron' misbehaviour. Boxing, the rugby codes, auto racing, and even tennis have all been sites for (often alcohol-fuelled) anti-social behaviour. While the incidents of physical violence have been limited, more common and pervasive forms of anti-social behaviour have included racial vilification, inappropriate sexual references to women, abuse towards officials and police, as well as vandalism and public lewdness. In short, anti-social behaviour in sport had not only become physically dangerous but had also compromised the legal rights of victimised spectators, reduced the support offered to sporting organisations, demanded significant resources from police and venues, led to economic losses through diminished gate receipts and venue damage, and undermined attempts to encourage people to attend and become involved in physical activity and sport.

Moreover, in a reversal of sport's much-lauded role modelling potential, the transgressions of high-profile athletes often encouraged young participants to conform to social sporting rituals involving the heavy consumption of alcohol and other high-risk behaviours.[33] In addition, generally liberal attitudes towards the inevitable association between sport and alcohol discouraged many parents from including their children in sporting activities. In addition, the celebrity and opinion-leader status of professional athletes often had a normalising effect upon public perceptions of sport as a convivial space to consume alcohol.[34]

Sport's problems do not end there. As we have demonstrated throughout this book, sport has rarely delivered on its promises when it comes to selling social development and justice issues messages. This lack of success has not been for the want of trying, especially over recent years when nearly every significant sporting competition was themed around a social cause. It can be put down to two factors. First, they have only an indirect link to their core role – or mission, if you like – which is to provide an array of organised physical activities for the enjoyment of participants. Second, they rarely have the resources – either financial or human – to deliver the messages in such a way that participants will engage with well-structured learning activities run by experience educators. Having a few enthusiastic players talking to schoolkids about character building, role modelling, ethics, civic responsibility, intersectionality, gender diversity, and critical race theory is just as likely to confuse as enlighten.

Fresh Ways of Managing Sport

So, where to from here? First, we acknowledge that it is far easier to snipe from the sidelines than offer constructive alternatives when thinking about how sport can better contribute to the quality of life and well-being of citizens.

But we also believe that governments have not always used 'evidence' to shape their sport development programmes but instead have utilised all those romanticised myths we discussed in earlier chapters to defend their policy initiatives. Veteran sport sociologist Jay Coakley viewed this approach to sport development as highly problematic since it failed to grasp the ways in which sport could – especially where neo-liberal values were driving organisational conduct and government policy[35] – undermine a community's quality of life.[36]

Despite the many challenges sport has faced in recent times, these myths have proved to be highly resilient, which is largely due to their 'narrative power'[37] and storytelling capability.[38] Not only are sporting stories seen to be intrinsically attention-grabbing (by taking people on emotional roller coaster journeys where both villains and heroes vie for the audience's attention), but they are also a catalyst for 're-storying' one's own life and thus reconstructing a roughly coherent identity and sense of self.'[39] They can reinforce neoliberal values by exploring the character-building qualities of competitive games, confirming the ways in which individual effort can deliver success, and highlighting the ways in which setbacks can be used as motivation to try harder. While sport's proponents think this is a good thing, critics believe it, once again, inculcates participants with all those individualistic, narcissistic, and materialistic values that make neo-liberalism harder to swallow.[40]

Finding a Way Out of the Sporting Jungle

Today's sporting myths thus have a life of their own, and we acknowledge that attempts to either discredit or dismantle them will take a lot of persuasive clout.[41] Neither are we ready to offer any explicit policy advice on how the harms that often follow can be better managed. It would take another book to examine all the alternatives, balance competing stakeholder demands, action them as programmes, and test them against current arrangements. But we also believe there are guiding principles that might deliver less corruption, lower rates of injury, and less psychological stress, while promoting diversity and inclusivity, all the while preserving the chaotic and seductive uncertainty of finely balanced physical contests that both players and fans crave.

First, there is a good case for arguing that sport-related policy should be underpinned by evidence collected from research studies that provide some form of quantitative measurement.[42] Our summary review demonstrated how a blend of systematically constructed studies can illuminate the crux of a problem and provide a clearer path for an effective solution while at the same time pointing to likely causal or correlated influences on the sporting experience.

Second, it makes sense to consider the views of all key stakeholders (and especially players and fans) when creating new sporting experiences and revamping old ones. There is a lot to be said for participants having their say. It also has a downside since it can end up being little more than a token gesture that allows business consultants and government bureaucrats to tick a few due-diligence boxes. Nevertheless, it has become a major talking point in the public policy arena, and in keeping with its growing popularity, it has been given intellectual respectability by being referred to as either post-positive participatory policy analysis[43] or an advocacy coalition frameworks approach.[44]

Third, it is important to consider not only the anticipated benefits but also the probable costs when assessing a proposed sport-related project.[45] This is obvious to disinterested observers but is not always addressed by those with a case to make. While some of the research studies we evaluated delivered outstanding exposés of the benefits of programme intervention, their overall value was diminished by either a deliberate or inadvertent disregard for the costs.[46]

Fourth, there has been a growing interest in the use of what might at first glance be relatively unimportant contextual factors to change the ways in which people behave and make decisions at both work and play. Under the theoretical umbrellas of behavioural economics and 'choice architecture,' subtle policy shifts have been increasingly used to 'nudge' people into actions deemed to be good for both individuals and society.[47] The aim was to replace coercive instruments like fines and suspensions with an array of finely crafted psychological inducements. There has been an enthusiastic flurry of activity, with all sorts of contextual adjustments being used to lower the incidence of player injuries, reduce alcohol consumption at match-day events, and manage the conduct of over-exuberant parents at their children's sporting competitions.[48] A lot of these 'choice architecture' initiatives have been innovative, but there is not a lot of evidence to suggest they can solve big sporting issues on a large scale.

Fifth, there is an emerging belief that governments, sporting bodies, and sport officials should take a leaf out of the sport mythmaking playbook, so to speak, by creating alternative narratives that include messages that privilege civility, responsible behaviour, and concern for the safety of others over conduct that intimidates opposition players and threatens their supporters. Storytelling has already been used in health-promoting messages as a way of replacing bad habits with good ones and dysfunctional relationships with supportive ones. It has been particularly valuable in promoting 'preventative' changes in health and physical activity behaviours,[49] especially where multi-media messages are constructed as personal life experiences.[50]

Yet we should not get too excited by the power of narratives to inspire others to do good things. They can just as easily be used to whip up a crowd, where emotion takes over space, reason gets pushed to the side, and violence is celebrated. Sport does this as well as any social institution. According to Christian Salmon, a columnist for the French daily newspaper Le Monde, contemporary storytelling was often used to hijack 'creative imagination' and debase the 'timeless human desire for narrative form.'[51] Salmon cited a number of illuminating examples where advertisers created brand images around a motley collection of simplistic archetypes, business managers invented slick anecdotes about corporate heroes to motivate employees to exploit themselves for the company, and 'spin doctors' constructed political lives as if they were a folk epic. Salmon viewed this new form of marketised 'storytelling machinery' as little more than an 'insidious form of oppression.'

Finally, there has been a call in some quarters for a radical change in the ways in which sport is played out, so to speak. Several critics of 21st century sport have argued for the development of a strong protest movement as a prelude to a complete overhaul of sport built on a foundation of 'values' renewal. Their aim was to shame sport into shaking off its hypermasculine traditions, doing something serious about the escalating cost of participant injuries, facing up to its ambivalence about violence, relaxing its obsession with the elimination of drugs, while also jettisoning its fantasy-like views about how team sports can magically make responsible men out of wayward boys and mature women out of rebellious girls.[52] There were also social justice activists who believed that what the sports world needed above all else was a 'cultural revolution' where there was more gender equity, inclusive engagement, spontaneous play and aesthetic movement, and fewer violent contests, physical abuse, racist chants, and instances of angry fans baying for blood.[53]

These arguments were challenging, since they asked sport officials to reconsider the ways sport was envisioned, organised, and played. They sought to re-introduce a 'sport for all' ethos in which playing around with friends, undertaking bushland journeys of self-discovery, or just having a good dose of vigorous exercise was no less socially valuable than securing a big win in a prestigious international sporting event.

Then there are the social justice warriors who reckoned a cultural revolution in sport would only come to pass if the whole economic base of western society was dismantled and anything to do with neo-liberalism was jettisoned. Accordingly, it would be replaced with an economic structure akin to socialism and a communitarian ethos built on collaboration and sharing. In this new world order, key industries would be state-owned, the rich would be taxed to within an inch of their lives, racism would be erased from the human psyche, gender equality would be achieved with room to spare, inclusion and diversity would be taken for granted, and every citizen would have a fundamental right to participate in harm-free physical recreation and sport activities without constraint.

Trapped in a Paradox of Sport

The above ruminations are broadly helpful, but none of them are likely to make a significant difference to the fundamental nature of sport around the planet. What is more, there are some aspects of sport that large numbers of followers don't want to change. Unfortunately, they often involve conduct that is risky and combative. Earlier we talked about the deep-seated need people – but mostly men – have, to either participate in or witness contests that involve a lot of physicality, courage, and related warrior like behaviour. It will always draw a crowd, but it can also lead to serious on-field injury and chaotic off-field violence. In these situations, the emotional rewards may be high, but so too will be the physical and social costs.

We thus find ourselves on the horns of a dilemma. If we sanitise sport by taking out the competitive physicality, fewer people are likely to engage with it,[54] but if we brutalise it, there will be increased harm done all round.[55] The only remedy is to manage it. Horse racing, boxing, and mixed martial arts are the exemplars here. If you did a benefit-cost analysis of these sports, you would probably ban them, safe in the knowledge that we would be collectively better off. But we also understand that if we ban things people enjoy, they will only go 'underground' and take on a black-market persona where crime becomes a perfect fit, and the social harms are only heightened. In these cases, the cure can be worse than the complaint.

There is, in our minds, only one way out of this conundrum, which is to re-regulate. But as we have indicated early on in this chapter, regulation can be corrupted by powerful lobby groups, and the accompanying economic, physical, and social costs can be horrifically high. But the alternative approach, where the free-market rules, would in our view, be catastrophic. All we can realistically ask for then is that governing bodies and governments take their responsibilities seriously and work on the assumption that when the costs of a sporting activity or enterprise outweigh the benefits, something is drastically wrong, and someone, somewhere, needs to do something about it.

A Window of Opportunity

We are left with only one workable solution to sport's problems, and it rests in the hands of government. A fresh form of external regulation that balances education and collaborative policy development, smart surveillance, effective enforcement, and proportionate penalties is, in our minds, the only viable way out. This is a depressing conclusion, since it contains nothing that is exciting or original. But like most other industries around the world, regulatory authorities are one of the few mechanisms that can protect society from the excesses of capitalism (especially where market power is centralised) and ensure the well-being of citizens.[56]

The final point to note – which is also somewhat depressing – is that sport will always impose significant physical, social, and emotional costs on the community. Without these risks and uncertainties, sport would lose its essential attractiveness. This is the nature of the beast, so to speak.[57] As we have argued throughout this book, all those external benefits that sport is supposed to deliver have also been massively exaggerated, which leaves sporting authorities saying things that are little more than wishful thinking. All we have left, then, is a reasonable expectation that regulators can limit the damage and help sport deliver a socially acceptable balance of costs, risks, and harms on one hand, and benefits, public value, and capital formation on the other. This may not be optimal, but it will guarantee sport a sustainable and satisfactory future. As for the precise nature of these fresh regulatory regimes, we will leave it for another day and another book.

Final Comments

Sport has been analysed in every imaginable way, and it would be reasonable to assume that everything we need to know about sport has been addressed. But having spent a lot of COVID-19 downtime reflecting on sport's recent progress and status and our own teaching and researching experience in the sport studies field, we concluded that there were still many knowledge gaps to be filled and vexing issues to be illuminated. There were, in our view, five aspects of sport that were still either not fully developed or in dispute. They became the driving force behind the writing of this book.

The first aspect is the **meaning and purpose of sport**. There is still a lack of clarity around what it is about sport that makes it such an important social institution. When observing sport at arm's length, it is often difficult to understand why so many people would want to spend so much time expending so much energy doing things that deliver not only memorable moments of ecstasy but a lot of emotional agony. We concluded that only a multipronged approach to sport engagement explains why it is taken so seriously.

The second aspect is the **essence of sport**. These days there is a tendency for governing bodies and social planners to prioritise inclusion, which makes sense when aiming to broaden the participation base. This has led to a situation where any time an activity has a hint of physical movement and/or the battle of wills, it is slotted under the sport banner. However, we have argued that sport is something quite special, and the more it opens itself to anything that moves or is contested, the more it takes away from its essence and 'perfectibility.'

The third aspect is the **celebratory mythologising of sport**. These are the beliefs and claims promulgated about sport's capacity to go beyond the here-and-now of sport experiences and the pleasure and joy it elicits and makes for more well-rounded citizens, stronger communities, and wealthier economies. These 'social benefits' are trumpeted far and wide as evidence of sport's unique ability to make society a better place. The benefits have a seductive quality to them, but we found they were often unaccompanied by supporting evidence. Because they have been cited so often, they are mostly left unquestioned and quickly become taken-for-granted assumptions. This is why we took readers through the origins of these celebratory beliefs, considered their status, and tested the claim against the research findings.

In the process, we have recast the celebratory beliefs about sport as a narrative – or storyline, if you like – that reads as follows:

> Sport not only delivers intrinsic pleasure, excitement, and moments of ecstasy, but also provides a vast array of positive 'spinoffs' that adds to its public value. These spinoffs include a strong ethical mindset, increased self-esteem, greater emotional resilience, improved educational attainment, the creation of positive role models, social cohesion, crime reduction, more connected communities, improvements in physical and mental health, increased productivity at work, an economic benefit to local communities, a more expansive recreational infrastructure, and a longer, more satisfying, and happier lifespan. Moreover, whenever waves of national pride wash over citizens there will be a legacy effect that can last for years. In short, sport, more than any other mass leisure activity, adds significant public value to society.

The fourth aspect is the **hyper-critical positioning of sport**. In this case, sport's critics aim to expose the risks, costs, and harms that accompany the sport experience while also refuting the views of hardened traditionists who argue that some 'biff and clout,' the occasional insult or slur, low-grade racism and sexism, competitive stress, residual cheating, and injury come with the territory. Critics also observe that many sport participants wallow in their misadventures by reinventing injury-related harms as badges of honour and have them take on 'war story' proportions. And not surprisingly, critics round out their inglorious view of sport by detailing its structural faults, where winners get all the glory and losers are left to fend for themselves.

Our narrative for the hyper-critical positioning of sport goes as follows:

> Most of the social benefits and spinoffs from sport are little more than comforting myths. They make intuitive sense since there is always anecdotal support and a story to tell. However, when the research is done, they do not stack up. What is more, there are many costs and harms which the myths camouflage. They begin with the material costs of playing, securing club membership, travelling to and from venues, and watching others play. Near the surface is a layer of drug-use, violence, bribery, corruption, and match-fixing, and below that a disturbing level of misogyny, homophobia, racism, and obnoxious misbehaviour by officials, parents, and fans. Deeper again is the taken-for-granted but increasingly heavy societal burden of dealing with physical injury, mental illness, and related disorders. In short, sport has a destructive propensity to strip away sport's public-value-building capacity.

These two competing narratives raise the following question: Is sport the key to a good society and thus deserves every dollar it gets from the government or is it an over-rated and poorly regulated institution that not only fails to deliver on many of its spinoff promises, but in the process, it also creates widespread levels of social chaos, physical harm, and psychological distress?

The fifth aspect is the **regulatory regimes that can impact sports**. There have been scattered accounts of how sport's governing bodies and relevant levels of government might use their regulatory tools to secure more of the social benefits that sport is supposed to deliver while also minimising the potential for social, economic, and political mayhem to occur. But outside of boxing and horse racing, there have been few attempts to apply the concept of 'market failure' to problematic sporting conduct. We were determined to fill the gap by not only exploring the ways sporting practices might fail the public interest test but also by formulating a regulatory mix that can best resolve the problem and improve citizen well-being. We did this by examining the ways in which rule modifications, bottom-up activism, cultural change, voluntary codes, and enforceable control-and-command style regulations might have had on the way things get done in sport, and especially how they may (or may not) lower risks and potential harms.

Having pondered over the above five aspects of sport and examined the ways in which they have shaped its organisation and practice, we concluded that it has come up short, with many fault lines exposed. Its capacity to build additional public value and strengthen society's stocks of capital has been diminished.

However, we also believe we have provided a roadmap for sport's rehabilitation as a crucial value-adding institution. In doing so, we invite readers to visualise a new, evidence-based sporting narrative that reshapes contemporary sport around an end-goal of enhancing citizen well-being.

Notes

1 Market failures occur where organisations and businesses have failed to bear the full cost of their production and instead passed part of it onto consumers. For example, a coal-fired power station that delivers electricity to its surrounding community is providing a benefit which consumers pay for. But in the delivery of the electricity, it may also be polluting the atmosphere with noxious chemicals and thus be causing widespread harm. As a result, the overall welfare of consumers has been eroded. The market has failed by delivering a sub-optimal outcome. Sport can create similar problems by organising risky events where the probability of being injured will be higher than normal. So, like the power station case, the external cost (in this instance, the injury) will be borne by the participant, while also diminishing their welfare and well-being. For an excellent primer on the causes and consequences of market failure, you should read Brian Andrew (2008). Market failure, government failure, and externalities in climate change mitigation: The case for a carbon tax, *Public Administration and Development*, 28: 393–401. Pages 394–398 explain all. For a fascinating examination of obesity as an example of market failure, see

Thomas Hemphill (2018). Obesity in America: A market failure? *Business and Society Review*, 123 (4): 619–630. According to Hemphill the research evidence says that a 'mix of institutional activities' will be necessary to solve America's 'epidemic levels of obesity and severe obesity.' They are (1) corporate social responsibility, (2) industry self-regulation, (3) social activism, and (4) government intervention.

2 Michael Long (2013). Sporting regulation: Lessons to be learned from other regulatory bodies? *Sports Pro Media*, 3 December.

3 For the definitive exploration of this notion, see Matthew Sinnicks (2022). On the analogy between business and sport: Towards an Aristotelian response to the market failures approach to business ethics, *Journal of Business Ethics,* 177: 49–61.

4 For all you need to know about self-regulation and how it works, see OECD (2015). Industry self-regulation: Role and use in supporting consumer interests, *OECD Digital Economy, Paper 247*, OECD Publishing.

5 A thorough exposition of external regulation and the different forms it can take is contained in UK National Audit Office (2021). *Good Practice Guidance Principles of Effective Regulation,* NAO. Good practice guidance Principles of effective regulation (nao.org.uk)

6 Values statements and codes of conduct have, in recent times, become important guiding principles for the good governance and management of sporting bodies around the world. For an excellent overview of these developments, see Els De Waegeneer, Jeroen Van De Sompele, and Annick Willem (2018). Ethical codes in sports organizations: Classification framework, content analysis, and the influence of content on cost effectiveness, *Journal of Business Ethics,* 136 (3): 587–598. Values statements and codes of conduct also rated highly in the Australian government's 2023 Sports Commission (ASC) document titled *Sport Governance Standards.* The ASC's other guiding principles for good governance and management were (1) a clear vision that informs strategy, (2) full documentation of duties, powers, roles, and responsibilities, (3) a diverse board and organisational membership, (4) processes that include transparency and accountability, (5) a system of risk management which protects members from harm, and (6) systems of internal review to ensure continuous improvement.

7 See, for example, Lisa Kihi (2023). Development of a national sport integrity system, *Sport Management Review,* 26(1): 24–47; and Jean-Loup Chappelet (2018). Beyond governance: The need to improve the regulation of international sport, *Sport and Society*, 21 (5): 724–734.

8 The 2023 regulations were set out in a 110-page document. The detail was frightening, but it was made very clear what teams had to do to participate in the competition.

9 New South Wales Parliament (2014). *Combat Sports Act 2013.*

10 Phil McManus, Glenn Albrecht, and Raewyn Graham (2013). *The Global Horseracing Industry: Social, Economic and Ethical Perspectives*, Routledge.

11 For more details see Graham Brooks, Azeem Aleem, and Mark Button (2016). *Fraud, Corruption and Sport.* Palgrave Macmillan: 107–122.

12 Mike Huggins (2003). *Horseracing and the British - 1919–39.* Manchester University Press.

13 See, for instance, Jason Proctor (2022). B.C. gaming inspector charged with accepting bribes in horse-racing investigation: 36 charges appear connected to 2019 investigation of activities at Vancouver's Hastings Racecourse, *CBC News*, 14 April.

14 It is generally agreed that the foundation components of successful regulatory schemes are: (i) clear public standards, (ii) an expedient, transparent, effective, and robust procedure to determine compliance, followed by (iii) a credible, meaningful sanction for breaching a regulation. By adopting these principles, sporting bodies are more likely to maintain their legitimacy and avoid intervention. But if they do not, they expose themselves to corrupt practices and direct government

intervention. An extended discussion on what makes for effective regulation, compliance, and enforcement is contained in Neil Gunningham (2015). Compliance, enforcement, and regulatory excellence, *Penn Program on Regulation*, PSU. Neil also makes the important point that there is one single best regulatory tool, since different settings, spaces, and sites will often require quite different regulatory responses.

15 One way of categorising sport's regulatory regimes is to view them as internally or externally managed, coercive or voluntary, and national or international in scope. This schema was adapted from Eric Windholz (2021). What can we learn from the regulation of sport? *Australia and New Zealand School of Government* (ANZSOG), 30 March.

16 One of the more scandalous incidents involved several professional football clubs in Greece where a multitude of 'financial crimes' were committed. For all the details, see Argyro Elisavet Manoli, Georgios Antonopoulos, and Michael Levi (2016). Football clubs and financial crimes in Greece, *Journal of Financial Crime,* 23 (3): 559–573. These 'financial crimes' included the issuing of ticket counterfeits, fake tax certificates, 'under the table' payments to players, money laundering, and match-fixing.

17 For a detailed discussion of regulatory failure, see Ernesto Dal Bo (2008). Regulatory capture: A review, *Oxford Review of Economic Policy*, 22 (2): 202–221. According to Dal Bo, regulatory failure mostly results from regulatory capture, which is the process by which 'big business' (and monopolies in particular) 'end up manipulating the [government] agencies that are supposed to control them.' This approach to regulatory failure was also adopted by Bandiera Rhiannon in her analysis of the Australian pharmaceutical sector. According to Rhiannon, the problem arose from the close relationship between the regulator and the regulated, which was labelled as a case of 'State-Corporate Harm.' The details are contained in Bandiera Rhiannon (2021). Marx, Foucault, and state-corporate harm: A case study of regulatory failure in Australian non-prescription medicine regulation, *Crime, Law, and Social Change*, 76 (2): 173–193. In the sports world, the best example of regulatory failure occurred leading up to the 2014 Sochi Winter Olympics when the Russian government did a secret deal with the national drug testing agency to manipulate the testing protocols for performance-enhancing substances. Corrupt practices by officials and players have also been a significant contributor to regulatory failure in sporting leagues and governing bodies.

18 Michael Long, Sporting regulation: Lessons to be learned from other regulatory bodies? *Sports Pro News*, 3 December.

19 Jean-Loup Chappelet and Michaël Mrkonjic (2019). Assessing sport governance principles and indicators. In *Research Handbook on Sport Governance*, Edward Elgar. See also Michaël Mrkonjic (2021). Good governance in sport strategies. Reforming organisations by adapting management competencies to governance functions, in *Good Governance in Sport*, Routledge. On p. 238 of 'Good Governance,' Mrkonjic called for a 'rethinking of the sport organisation' by first investigating the various forms that governance structures and functions might take, and second, questioning the management competencies needed to reform a sport organisation to meet a good governance strategy.

20 For a revealing expose of the sport doping 'industry,' see L. Paoli and A. Donati (2013). *The Sports Doping Market: Understanding Supply and Demand, and the Challenges of their Control*, Springer.

21 For an excellent overview of the sport and corruption problem, see Wladimir Andreff (2019). *An Economic Roadmap to the Dark Side of Sport Volume II: Corruption in Sport*, Springer.

22 When it comes to sport's commercialisation, there is still vigorous disagreement on what it has contributed to the sporting experience of players and fans. In a recent study on the response of fans to sport's commercial growth, the findings revealed a lot of fan ambivalence. On one hand, fans appreciated the vast improvements in stadia design and comfort, but they were also concerned with the 'Disneyfication' of the game, with nearly everything that moved being branded, the 'Celebritisation' of players, and the consequent undermining of 'team authenticity.' These and many other issues were examined in Erik Winell, John Armbrecht, Erik Lundberg, and Jonas Nilsson (2023). How are fans affected by the commercialization of elite sports? A review of the literature and a research agenda, *Sport, Business and Management: An International Journal*, 13 (1): 118–137.

23 This issue was addressed in Arnout Geeraert (2019). The limits and opportunities of self-regulation: Achieving international sport federations' compliance with good governance standards, *European Sport Management Quarterly*, 19 (4): 520–538. Geeraert concluded that 'good governance standards and effective compliance in international sport federations required either 'co-regulation' – where self- regulation's persuasion and management mechanisms were supplemented by sanctions implemented by public and/or civil society actors – or 'meta-regulation' – where public actors imposed a minimum standard for self-regulation that included 'robust monitoring and sanctioning mechanisms.' Otherwise, some form of unethical or corrupt conduct would be likely.

24 A good example of how a sport-based government intervention can assist the attainment of a social policy objective occurred in Sweden in the 2010s when a 'Midnight football' programme was introduced in order to get young – mainly single – and marginalised males to engage in an evening team sport programme. The aim was to provide wayward youth with an activity that would not only occupy their time in useful ways and build their self-esteem but also lower the probability of them becoming petty criminals. This programme was magnificently reported in David Ekholm and Magnus Dahlstedt (2022). *Social Policy: Midnight Football and the Governing of Society*, Taylor & Francis Group.

25 According to medical authorities around the world, the number of documented concussions will continue to rise with increased participation of youth in sports as well as improved concussion awareness and management. In addition, in the United States, concussion litigation became highly contentious because of the 2009 Lystedt case, where a player who sustained a head-to-ground injury during a football game continued to play despite exhibiting confusion and memory difficulty. There were no medical staff in attendance who could have done an assessment. As it turned out, the player had life-saving emergency surgery that left him severely disabled. As a consequence of this case, concussion legislation was introduced into all 50 American states. For more details, see Matthew Provencher, Rachel Frank, Daniel Shubert, Anthony Sanchez, and Colin Murphy (2019). Concussions in sports, *Orthopedics* (Online), 42 (1): 12–21; and Kathleen Bachynski and Daniel Goldberg (2014). Youth sports and public health: Framing risks of mild traumatic brain injury in American football and ice hockey, *The Journal of Law, Medicine & Ethics*, 42 (3): 323–333.

26 Danielle Kamis, Thomas Newmark, Daniel Begel, and Ira Glick (2016). Cheating and sports: History, diagnosis and treatment, *International Review of Psychiatry*, 28 (6): 551–555.

27 For a stark international analysis, see Stacey Steele and Hayden Opie (eds.) (2017). *Match-fixing in Sport: Comparative Studies from Australia, Japan, Korea and Beyond*, Routledge. Some excellent case studies are contained in chapter 3 of Nic Groombridge (2016). *Sports Criminology: A Critical Criminology of Sport and Games*, Bristol University Press & Policy Press. The relationship between

match-fixing and gambling is succinctly addressed in Tom Serby (2012). Gambling related match-fixing: A terminal threat to the integrity of sport? *The International Sports Law Journal*, (1–2): Online publication.

28 For an excellent overview of the problem and how widespread it is, see David Alaminos and Manuel Ángel Fernández (2019). Why do football clubs fail financially? A financial distress prediction model for European professional football industry. *Plos One*, 14 (12): Online publication. According to the authors, low liquidity, high leverage, poor sports performance, and the small size of the club market were the best predictors of the distress of football clubs.

29 In 2019, the World Anti-Doping Agency (WADA) banned Russia from all international sporting competitions – including the Olympics – for four years over doping non-compliance. In 2020, when Russia appealed the decision, the [international] Court of Arbitration for Sport reduced the ban to two years, and Russia was free to engage in international competition in 2023.

30 An excellent overview of corrupt practices in sport is available in Adam Master (2015). Corruption in Sport: From the playing field to the field of policy, *Policy and Society* 34 (2): 111–123. Master provocatively argued that international sport had, by the second decade of the new millennium, entered a fifth evolutionary trend – criminalisation – which followed on from: (1) de-amateurisation at the turn of the 20th century, (2) medicalisation since the 1960s, (3) politicisation since the 1970s, and (4) commercialisation since the 1990s. So, by 2022 it was not surprising to find that a book was published that devoted itself to an analysis of the criminology of sport. The title was *Sport and Crime: Towards a Critical Criminology of Sport*, and the authors were Peter Millward, Jan Andre, Lee Ludvigsen, and Jonathan Sly, and the publisher was Routledge.

31 This issue was cleverly explored in Argyro Elisavet Manoli, Comille Bandura, and Paul Downward (2020). Perceptions of integrity in sport: Insights into people's relationship with sport, *International Journal of Sport Policy and Politics*, 12 (2): 207–220. The authors found that even though sport [was] viewed as 'corrupt and unable to improve, its perceived role as a mechanism for social outcomes…remained unaffected, creating a potentially vicious circle in which sport [had] little to no pressing urgency or strong motivation to protect its integrity.'

32 See, for example, Holly Knapton, Lisa Espinosa, Henk Meier, Emma Bäck, and Hanna Bäck (2018). Belonging for violence: Personality, football fandom, and spectator aggression, *Nordic Psychology*, 4: 278–289; and Steven Block and Eric Lesneskie (2012). A thematic analysis of spectator violence at sporting events in North America, *Deviant Behavior*, 39 (9):1–13.

33 Anders Sønderlund, Kerry O'Brien, Peter Kremer, Bosco Rowland, Florentine De Groot, Petra Staiger, Lucy Zinkiewicz, and Peter Miller (2014). The association between sports participation, alcohol use and aggression and violence: A systematic review, *Journal of Science and Medicine in Sport*, 17 (1): 2–7.

34 See, for example, Richard Purves, Nathan Critchlow, and Angus Bancroft (2020). Sport Fan Attitudes on Alcohol: Insights from a Survey of Football Supporters in Scotland and England, *Journal of Sport and Social Issues*, 46 (2): Online publication. However, a recent Norwegian study found that while a normalising effect occurred, it did not lead to increased levels of alcohol consumption. For more details see Geir Brunborg, Torleif Halkjelsvik, and Inger Moan (2022). Sports participation and alcohol use revisited: A longitudinal study of Norwegian postmillennial adolescents, *Journal of Adolescence*: 587–599.

35 For strong critiques of the ways in which neoliberalism had supposedly destroyed the health and well-being of communities, particularly those who were already disadvantaged, see Kiffer Card and Kirk Hepburn (2023). Is neoliberalism killing

us? A cross-sectional study of the impact of neoliberal beliefs on health and social wellbeing in the midst of the COVID-19 pandemic, *International Journal of the Social Determinants of Health and Health Services*, 53 (3): 363–373; Elizabeth Sweet (2018). Like you failed at life: Debt, health, and neoliberal subjectivity, *Social Science and Medicine*, 212: 86–93; Marian Peacock, Paul Bissell, and Jenny Owen (2014). Dependency denied: Health inequalities in the neo-liberal era, *Social Science and Medicine*, 118: 173–180; and Stephen Nkansah-Amankra, Samuel Agbanu and Reuben Miller (2013). Disparities in health, poverty, incarceration, and social justice among racial groups in the United States: A critical review of evidence of close links with neoliberalism, *International Journal of Health Services*, 43 (2): 217–240.

36 For an astute discussion of sporting myths, see Jay Coakley (2015). Assessing the sociology of sport: On cultural sensibilities and the great sport myth, *International Review for the Sociology of Sport*, 50 (4–5): 402–406. Coakley argued that sport was underpinned by one dominant and overarching myth, which said that sport was inherently pure and good, and thus, as a matter of course, delivered vast amounts of public value, social utility, and societal capital. He called it the Great Sport Myth (GSM). Coakley also proposed that sport's key stakeholders (its administrators, coaches, players, volunteer officials, medical and para-medical support staff, the media, corporate partners, fans, and especially government and its agencies) were instrumental in not only supporting GSM but also transmitting it to future sporting generations. Coakley noted, though, that the GSM was a reactionary force, since it was underpinned by a belief in the status quo, where a virtuous circle of participant growth, government support, professionalism, fan involvement, and corporate engagement delivered benefits to everyone. Coakley detected a massive downside, where most of the benefits accrued to the corporate sector and the costs were shouldered by participants and fans. He additionally noted that the GSM had, by masking this reality, both enabled the 'ruling elites' to 'appropriate public money for private gain' and placed barriers in front of critical researchers who wanted to 'facilitate social change and activism.'

37 Results from a laboratory-based experiment involving 554 subjects found that narratives were processed more fluently (and more easily) than non-narratives. In addition, when the narrative processing had been completed, persuasion became more likely. For all the details, see Olivia Bullock, Hillary Shulman, and Richard Huskey (2021). Narratives are persuasive because they are easier to understand: Examining processing fluency as a mechanism of narrative persuasion, *Frontiers in Communication*, 6 (7): Online publication.

38 Cited in Guy Hansen (2023). Tales from a Sporting Nation, in Robert Nichols (ed), *Grit and Gold: Tales from a Sporting Nation*, National Library of Australia: 4–5.

39 David Carless and Kitrina Douglas (2008). Narrative, identity and mental health: How men with serious mental illness re-story their lives through sport and exercise, *Psychology of Sport and Exercise*, 9 (5): 576–594. Carless and Douglas identified three narrative types underlying participants' talk about sport and exercise. The first was an action narrative about 'going places and doing stuff'; the second was an achievement narrative about accomplishment through effort, skill, or courage; and the third was a relationship narrative of shared experiences to talk about with others.

40 Many researchers have concluded that using neo-liberal values to guide one's life journey can be problematic. See, for instance, Julia Becker, Lea Hartwich, and Alexander Haslam (2021). Neoliberalism can reduce well-being by promoting a sense of social disconnection, competition, and loneliness, *British Journal of Social Psychology*, 60: 947–965. One researcher went so far as to argue that neo-liberal values, especially their emphasis on individualism, had paradoxically led to a more punitive society that 'came down hard' on the 'deviant few who wilfully choose to

offend.' While this meant it provided more safe spaces to the innocent 'victims,' it still held to the view that competition was a 'virtue' and its results were generally more positive than negative. For more on the relationship between neoliberalism, competition, crime, and victimhood, see Antonia Porter (2020). *Prosecuting Domestic Abuse in Neoliberal Times: Amplifying the Survivor's Voice*, Palgrave Macmillan, especially the chapter on 'Neoliberalism, the CPS and Tenacious Domestic Abuse Prosecutions': 79–117. There is also a strong argument in support of the view that neoliberalism and the cult of individualism will 'ultimately damage kinship, collectivism, altruistic tendencies, and social compassion.' For a detailed exposition of this claim, see Jon Dean (2015). Volunteering, the market, and neoliberalism, *People, Place and Policy*, 9 (2): 139–148.

41 Myths, and their accompanying narratives, provide a seductive psychological tool for making sense of the world. Sporting myths are especially potent since they take what is an often ephemeral and fleeting experience and transform it into something that we believe makes both participants and the broader community better off. But it does not end there since the accompanying stories are nearly always subject to narrative bias. This means that information that challenges the myth is quickly jettisoned, while anecdotes that give weight to the myth become embedded in the story. For an instructive discussion of storytelling and the risk of narrative bias, see Michael Dahlstroma (2021). The narrative truth about scientific misinformation, *PNAS*, 118 (15): Online publication.

42 The idea that the best policy options will be arrived at when a large part of the evidence is centred on hard measurement, with judgement and intuition given secondary weight only, was persuasively argued by Ray Pawson (2006). *Evidence-based Policy: A Realist Perspective*. Sage. The thrust of his argument is contained in pp. 1–18 and pp. 178–180.

43 Participatory policy analysis is fully explained in Randy Clemons and Mark McBeth (2020). *Public Policy Praxis; A Case Approach for Understanding Policy and Analysis*, Routledge: 210–213. A lot of time is also spent distinguishing between positivist (rational and systematic) policy analysis and post-positivist (judgemental and interpretive) policy analysis.

44 For an excellent discussion of how the advocacy coalition framework can be applied to sport policy formulation, see Barrie Houlihan (2005). Public sector sport policy: Developing a framework for analysis, *International Review for the Sociology of Sport*, 40 (2): 163–185.

45 Despite its limitations, cost-benefit analysis remains a powerful tool for both analysing the potential potency of new policy options and evaluating the effectiveness of existing policies. For a full and clear account of the theories underpinning it and its practical application, you can do no better than read chapter 1 of Anthony Boardman, David Greenberg, Aiden Vining, and David Weimer (2021). *Cost-Benefit Analysis: Concepts and Practices 5th Edition*, Cambridge University Press.

46 Cost-benefit analysis also forces policymakers to search for facts and not take the easy way out by defaulting to values and beliefs about what should happen or what people would like to see happen. The sporting myths we have addressed in previous chapters fit perfectly with this approach to policy making. Cost-benefit analysis is, though, unashamedly technocratic, asking the following question: What are the bad and good effects of imaginable problems? If you want to read a highly persuasive defence of cost-benefit analysis and why it should be part of every policy designer's toolkit you should read Cass Sunstein (2019). *The Cost-Benefit Revolution*, The MIT Press.

47 One of the most interesting early books written on this was Richard Thaler, and Cass Sunstein (2009). *Nudge: Improving Decisions about Health, Wealth and Happiness*, Penguin Books. They talk a lot about why and how people make irrational decisions

and frequently explain them by referring to procrastination, overconfidence in one's abilities, cognitive biases, herd mentality, and loss aversion. A variety of policy approaches are explained in detail in Erik Angner (2021). *A Course in Behavioral Economics 3rd edition,* Bloomsbury.

48 A smorgasbord of policy options is contained in Hannah Josepha, Rachel Altman, Morris Altman, and Benno Torgler (2021). *Behavioural Sports Economics: A Research Companion*, Routledge. Some interesting insights can also be gleaned from the criminal justice policy literature. See, for instance, Matthew Davies and Simon Ruda (2023). Reflections on applying behavioural insights to crime: A guide for behavioural scientists and criminologists in search of policy unicorns, *Behavioural Public Policy* 7 (3): 744–757. The authors identified five 'tenets' to positive behavioural change in crime prevention settings, all of which can be applied to the sporting sphere. They are (1) increasing the effort required to act in harmful ways (e.g. installing steering column locks); (2) increasing the risk of being 'found out' (e.g. putting burglar alarms in place); (3) reducing potential rewards (e.g. 'marking' property that might be stolen); (4) reducing the likelihood of interpersonal provocation (e.g. providing separate seating for rival sporting team supporters); and (5) removing the opportunities for making excuses for invasive and/or harmful behaviour (e.g. putting 'private property' or other restrictive signage in place). If you want to read something that has a health, fitness, and exercise slant, we suggest Christina Roberto and Ichiro Kawachi (2015). *Behavioral Economics and Public Health*, Oxford University Press.

49 For an incisive explanation of the persuasive powers of narratives in health and physical activity settings, see Lauren B. Frank, Sheila T. Murphy, Joyee S. Chatterjee, Meghan B. Moran, and Lourdes Baezconde-Garbanati (2015). Telling stories, saving lives: creating narrative health messages, *Health Communication*, 30 (2): 154–163.

50 Recent research has shown that personal experiences and related anecdotes can have positive influences when used as (1) 'inspiration and empowerment tools to stimulate policy inquiries,' (2) 'educational and awareness tools to initiate policy discussions and gain public support,' and (3) 'advocacy and lobbying tools to formulate, adopt, or implement policy. For a detailed discussion around these points, see Yuyan Shen, Vivian Sheer, and Ruobing Li (2015). Impact of narratives on persuasion in health communication: A meta-analysis, *Journal of Advertising*, 44 (2): 105–113.

51 All is explained in Christian Salmon (2017). *Storytelling: Bewitching the Modern Mind*, Verso Books, Jonathan Gottschall said much the same in his 2022 publication *The Story Paradox: How Our Love of Storytelling Builds Societies and Tears them Down*, Little Brown. Accordingly, the 'very tradition that built human civilization' has also been used to drag people apart – especially around gender and race – and manipulate each other by 'circumventing rational thought.' Gottschall concluded that 'behind all civilization's greatest ills environmental destruction, runaway demagogues, warfare you will always find the same master factor: a mind-disordering story.'

52 These sentiments sound good, but as long-time sport academic and researcher Douglas Hartmann noted, while 'activism in and through sport is particularly effective in communicative and dramaturgical ways… it can be difficult to move from protest to actual social change.' Cited in Douglas Hartmann (2023). Sport, social movements, and athlete activism, in Lawrence Wenner (ed.) *The Oxford Handbook of Sport and Society*, Oxford University Press: 586.

53 See, for example, the writings in Thomas Carter, Daniel Burdsey, and Mark Doidge (eds). (2019). *Transforming Sport: Knowledges, Practices, Structures*, Routledge.

54 As we have repeatedly argued in this book, this is the unfortunate reality of contemporary sport. But it should not be surprising since sport is essentially about adversarial competitions and contests where physically overpowering one's opponent, securing victory, and getting the 'spoils' is the primary goal. According to critics, this is nothing more than a reflection of 'capitalist ideology,' where the logic of sport 'celebrates individual success over collective endeavour, competition over solidarity, and violence and aggression over contemplation and reflection.' For further discussion of this point, see Ben Carrington (2023). Sport, ideology and power, in Lawrence Wenner (ed.), *The Oxford Handbook of Sport and Society*, Oxford University Press: 54–55.

55 There are, as it turns out, many sporting paradoxes. For example: It can be initially playful, spontaneous, and autonomous, but often ends up being deadly serious and highly regimented. It can be good for the health and well-being of participants, but it can also kill them. It unites diverse communities, but it can also inflame the differences between them. Its traditions maintain participant and fan loyalty, but their inertia can be an impediment to commercial growth. Gender-specific sporting contests not only provide women with spaces to compete internationally but also signal inferior status when compared to male-only sports. It provides space for seeking perfection, but an obsessive need to be perfect can lead to stress, burnout, and early retirement. Finally, the things that sporting crowds do to build a memorable at-ground atmosphere are the same things that produce serious levels of violence. Some of these paradoxes are expertly discussed in Hans Næss (2018). Stories and stakeholders: How to explore the paradox of commercialism in sports, *Sport in Society*, 21(2): 201–214; and Ashley Rogers, Miriam Snellgrove, and Samantha Punch (2022). Between equality and discrimination: The paradox of the women's game in the mind-sport bridge, *World Leisure Journal*, 64 (4): 342–360.

56 Government regulation has its critics, but for the most part is viewed as a crucial tool for ensuring the business sector (including not-for-profit enterprises in and around the sporting sector) optimises its contribution to society and enhances the well-being of citizens. For a broad discussion of what is now called 'regulatory capitalism,' see A. Asquer (2017). Theories of regulation, *Studies in the Political Economy of Public Policy, Online publication*; Howard Beales, Jerry Brito, J. Kennerly Davis Jr, Christopher DeMuth, Donald Devine, Susan Dudley, Brian Mannix, and John O. McGinnis (2017). Government regulation: The good, the bad, & the ugly, *Regulatory Transparency Project of the Federalist Society*, 12 June. https://regproject.org/wp-content/uploads/RTP-Regulatory-Process-Working-Group; and Andrei Leal (2021). Collaborative regulation: Which is the role of the regulator in collaborative regulation, *The Law, State and Telecommunications Review*, 13 (1): 40–69.

57 Studies have shown that men who played competitive sport in an aggressive manner 'were rated as the most desirable partner for all levels of relationship commitment, including both short- and long-term relationships.' For a fascinating account of this phenomena, see G. Brewer and Sharon Howarth (2012). Sport, attractiveness and aggression, *Personality, and Individual Difference*, 21: 640–643.

Index

Note: **Bold** indicates tables in the text and page numbers followed by "n" refer to end notes.

For Product Safety Concerns and Information please contact our EU representative GPSR@taylorandfrancis.com
Taylor & Francis Verlag GmbH, Kaufingerstraße 24, 80331 München, Germany

www.ingramcontent.com/pod-product-compliance
Lightning Source LLC
LaVergne TN
LVHW010937110826
845149LV00013B/2646

* 9 7 8 1 0 3 2 9 0 2 9 1 3 *